DEPRESSION

EXPOSED

A Spiritual Enlightenment on a Dark Subject

By

DR. BELINDA G. MOSS

xulon PRESS

Depression Exposed: A Spiritual Enlightenment on a Dark Subject
by Belinda G. Moss, Ph.D.

Printed in the United States of America

ISBN 978-1-60266-823-2

www.xulonpress.com

Table of Contents

Acknowledgements

*M*y deepest gratitude to God, the Father, for making my life like a dream. You have been patient with me throughout the years and because of your undying love and faithfulness, You can now partake of the fruit of your labor. I am now postured to be an instrument of righteousness; one who can advance the Kingdom of God through helping your people get and stay free. I love you with all my heart, all of my soul, all of my mind, and all of my strength.

I also thank you, Perry, the man of my dreams, my husband, my love, and my covenant partner. It is because of your steadfast determination to be a true man of God that I am the woman I am. You have helped me in ways that only the Father can reward. I am free because of you and for that I am forever grateful. I love you with all my heart and I look forward to living the rest of my life in your loving arms.

To my loving daughter, Dawn, thank you for being so resilient since what seems like birth. You made single parenting easy and I, too, celebrate your accomplishments. I especially thank you for giving me such a wonderful son-in-law, Sebastian, and the apple of my eye, my granddaughter, Breanna Octavia. I love you sincerely.

To my family, friends, and intercessors, thank you for being supportive during this Kingdom assignment. Your love and prayers have helped me through this process and our Father, nor I, shall forget your labor of love.

A special thank you to A.A.S. for your untiring efforts to make my life easier.

Lastly, to the proofreaders of this book, thank you so much for volunteering your time to assist me in making this book of Kingdom proportion. My joy is knowing that every person who is set free by reading this book will be added to your list of deeds for God.

Introduction

*I*t's been ten years since my last bout with depression which persisted over a twenty year period. Being released from its powerful grip has been one of the greatest and most rewarding triumphs in my life. Not only am I totally free from depression, but I am now in a position to help millions of people, both Christians and non-Christians, to be delivered from this powerful oppressive spirit. So why did it take so long to write this book? Because until this time, this book has been in seed form. The scripture says, first the blade, then the ear, then the full corn in the ear. This seed has been germinating and I can truly say, it's harvest time for the people of God.

So, you are now holding this book. Chances are you or someone close to you has suffered with depression and if you have not received information like that which will be revealed in this book, more than likely it continues to have its grip on you or someone close to you.

Does the term "black cloud" sound familiar? Anyone who has had a serious struggle with depression is familiar with this term. Why? Because when the *feelings* associated with depression surface it seems like a black cloud is hovering over you; something evil relentlessly controlling you, unwilling to release you, taunting you throughout the day with thoughts that propel you to sink further into oblivion. You lose energy, develop unusual eating patterns, become somewhat of a recluse, resuming only because "you have to earn a paycheck," and produce Oscar-like performances because you don't want anyone to know what you're experiencing. You are living a quietly desperate life. Sounds familiar? That my friend is **depression**.

The strange thing is, not all depression is caused by anxiety, divorce, death, loss of employment, concern over children, etc. In fact, it doesn't take much before it rears its ugly head. You went to sleep the night before, but when you awakened, that cloud was evident; the pressure was there; the venom spewing from this invisible but real enigma, bombarding you with thoughts, debilitating you, causing you to take refuge in your bed or behind closed doors for hours, exclaiming, "here we go again."

And somehow we think that only women suffer from depression. The truth is although most research shows that women are much more likely than men to suffer from depression, men also have trouble escaping its hold. It is often overlooked in men because men are oftentimes reluctant to let their true emotions show; they think it will make them seem like a wimp, rather than the machismo they have been trained to sport. If all of the men who suffer from depression were to step forward, chances are there wouldn't be a lot of difference in the statistics when compared with the number of women who also have depression.

So, this book is not written to women only. It is written to anyone who has been controlled by this evil force and anyone who wants to be delivered once and for all from depression or any oppressive spirit that is keeping you from enjoying the good life. Believe it or not, life is supposed to be sweat less; life *can* be good.

My approach: First, I want to introduce you to me, a successful, solid, loving and ecstatically happy individual who escaped the claws of depression. But it was a journey, a very long and painful journey, one that you can circumvent if you take heed to what's written in this book. After years of intense internal suffering, I literally drew a line in the sand and declared depression off limits. Now, I have been living totally free of its grip for over 10 years. My intent is to demonstrate that if I can be free, you too can be totally free.

Secondly, one of the most powerful ways to defeat depression is to understand it. Knowledge is power and understanding is a wellspring of life to those who find it (Proverbs 16:22). So, like peeling an onion, I will expose depression layer by layer until we reach the core. Therefore, even though I am a Christian, and this book will be written from a spiritual perspective, I deem it necessary to explore depression both clinically, or what I call from a world's perspective, and spiritually. Why? Because clinically, there is a plethora of information defining depression, its symptoms, and treatment. On the internet alone there were over 80 million hits on the subject of depression. However, none of the clinical information offers the hope that the Word of God provides, thus the spiritual perspective. Proverbs 3:13 says, "Happy (blessed, fortunate, enviable) is the man who finds skillful and godly Wisdom, and the man who gets understanding [drawing it forth from God's Word and life's experiences]" (Amplified Version).

Lastly, when all the layers have been removed, and the root cause of depression is exposed, you will have a prescription for total life prosperity; a life you deserve and were predestined to have.

This is not a religious book but a book on emancipation using Godly principles. These principles can be used by anyone and will work for anyone who will apply them. I'm living the success of this information today; literal proof of its effectiveness.

The Scripture says Christ has set us free to live a free life (Galatians 5:1). You do not have to suffer from depression another day. However, choosing a life free of depression is a choice. It's a decision that you and you alone must make. Commit to read this book in its entirety and together, let's add another free soul now available for maximum use in the Kingdom of God. Come walk with me as I expose this oppressive spirit called ***Depression***.

My Story   *1*

CRYE

So how did it all begin? How did depression find its target in me, an educated and successful career military officer, humanitarian, minister, and prolific orator empowering thousands globally? It was quite simple. I never dealt with my stuff.

As a child and adolescent I was never happy with myself. In some way, like most people, I longed for acceptance. I have always been fairly intelligent so that was never a factor. However, I was never pleased with my physical appearance. So, I used my intelligence to mask my real insecurities. Very early in my life I dealt with low self-esteem, no self-concept, insecurities and an inferiority complex, all which later led to suicide ideation. I was a child with insecurities and left unattended, I developed into a woman with insecurities. I felt so misunderstood. Most of my adult life was spent meditating on "me." I confessed daily that "no one understood me." I felt so alone. I journaled every day (many years later I read that journal and quickly realized it was by the grace of God that I survived this onslaught; my thoughts were hopelessly deranged).

Consider my resume: A highly educated woman, I graduated with honors on all my undergraduate, graduate and post graduate degrees. I was successful in my military career. As an Intelligence

Officer, I was handpicked to brief visiting high ranking officers and dignitaries including members of the House Appropriations Committee and a host of International leaders. As a therapist, I received accolades for facilitating conduct-disordered youth—gang members who others had discarded. As a Minister of the Gospel, I was the pastor of three churches, one of which God used me to build from the ground up in Negrito Village in the Republic of the Philippines. I am known still today as Pastor Belinda, "the one who built a church for the most impoverished Negritos in Angeles City." Consequently, my work there was featured on CBS' 60 Minutes. I have ministered globally changing the lives of thousands.

Sounds fabulous, huh? However, inside I was empty and desperately sad. But I was good, I masked it well. No one knew that this brilliant and loving woman was a fatality waiting to happen. Like the Pharisees, I was well polished on the outside but I was a pretender, *"... (hypocrites)! For you are like tombs that have been whitewashed, which look beautiful on the outside but inside are full of dead men's bones..." (Matthew 23:27, Amplified).*

As time progressed, even though I was a military officer and active leader in the church, the noise of the enemy was becoming louder than any other voice around. I had become severely depressed. I contemplated seeking help from a mental health professional because life was becoming unbearable. Notice I pondered a secular helps profession over the church. Why? The teaching at the church I attended offered no solutions to my internal wars. However, I knew that I could not seek professional help because the military thought it made one susceptible to espionage, and therefore participating in therapy could cost me my military career. So, I understood that this was a secret I had to keep bottled up. Living a double life was literally killing me. I coined the phrase "Life is a B-52;" one of the largest bomber aircraft in the military arsenal. Life was hard and life was miserable.

One day, I decided enough was enough. I needed an escape and committing suicide seemed like my only hope. So, I digested a bottle of pills only to wake up a few hours later feeling physically sick. My first attempt at suicide was a failure. This really messed with my head.

Somehow I survived those initial years of despair, but because I was ignorant of depression and the root causes, my life paralleled a volcanic eruption on the horizon. I made a terrible mistake by marrying a man I thought was sent to me by God. Years later, I realized it was a familiar spirit that had ministered to me (I'll discuss more on familiar spirits later); nevertheless, the failure of this marriage thrust me into a deeper depression.

While we were married, my ex-husband became an adulterer and returned to using drugs. His elusive behavior nearly cost me my life. By this time I was promoted among the ranks in the military and this double life became increasingly confusing. I wore so many masks that I began showing up donning the wrong one. Who was I? I certainly didn't know.

Satan took advantage of my undisciplined mind and uncontrolled emotions. Previously, he provided little adversity because I was digging my own grave. The satanic attacks intensified and the volcano was about to erupt. While married to my ex-husband, he developed HIV, the virus that causes Acquired Immune Deficiency Syndrome (AIDS). By the grace of God I never contracted AIDS, and some twenty years later I have been cleared by the physicians to suspend any further testing (of course the Great Physician cleared me from that some 2,000 years ago).

After four years of hell on earth, I finally divorced my husband. Let me add a side note here. Although the evidence was clear that I made a mistake by marrying my ex-husband, **religion** kept me trapped for four years. I believed that because I was a minister, I could not get a divorce and other preachers supported this untruth. I was informed that I had to "endure this hardship as a first class soldier so God could get the glory."

When I finally divorced my ex-husband, the Lord said to me, "What took you so long?" Of course, the delay was because I thought "I was suffering for the Lord." The Lord corrected my theology and I pray it corrects yours. I realize this opens up a whole bucket of worms, but I felt it necessary to mention this one point, because religion will kill you. It killed Jesus. You were born by the Word of God and must live by the Word of God, not someone's opinion. If you are in this situation, seek the Lord and He will answer you.

My Date with a .357 Magnum

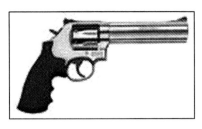

During those four years, life became extremely difficult and the plan of the enemy finally matured. I decided once again that enough was enough. After my divorce and my daughter left to attend college, I was being stalked by an intruder. My best friend wanted to assist me so she gave me a .357 Magnum to protect myself. Neither of us knew that this was the means by which the enemy would entice me to take my life. Reports indicate that the Magnum is "a powerful revolver with great precision and will happily shoot ammunition and return good results." Its precision was irrelevant because my plan was straight to the head. One night while all alone and having a serious pity party, I took the cold barrel of the .357 Magnum to my head and recited these few words, "Lord, please take care of my daughter when I'm gone." Once again, the mercy of God prevailed; I was gripped by fear and could not pull the trigger. Although depression still prevailed over the years, this was my last suicide attempt.

Although my military career continued to flourish, and I was still being used mightily by God, I sank further into depression. After returning from ministering life-changing messages, I would curl up in my hotel room and cry, "What about me?" I saw hundreds, thousands even, get free through the words that were released from my lips, yet, I could not shake this black cloud, so I continued with the façade, until I met Major Perry Moss, Jr.

Harvest Time

I married Major Moss several years after my divorce, but after a few months of dating him. It was my husband's resilience in the Word of God that was instrumental in my emancipation. He quickly noticed this sharp poster board military officer and well-respected Preacher had problems. He experienced the mood swings, the days of despair when I reclined in our bedroom and the frequent calls to the office feigning illness. One day, he confronted me about this behavior. His words were, "Woman, you are a Holy Ghost filled woman of God, you better start doing something about this depression." He told me I needed to "Get in the Word and build up myself." We have a bonus room over our garage. He suggested that I go "upstairs and pray in the spirit (in tongues) until I got delivered."

Initially, I think I acquiesced out of anger (he's only been saved a New York minute, I surmised and he's going to tell me what to do?) still I went because he refused to attend my pity parties (I had to celebrate alone).

Out of desperation I increased my study in the Word of God and went "upstairs" daily, whether I felt like it or not. I didn't feel a thing but I kept praying, every day; every time depression reared its ugly head; every time I felt the presence of the "black cloud." Gradually the depression began to lift. The occurrence was less often and after several months I finally got free. Remember, knowledge is power. I began to recognize the symptoms and I learned how to fight; I no longer accepted its invitation and forceful entries. Today, I am **totally** free from depression and have written this book to help you.

Before I proceed, let me explain briefly about praying in the spirit or praying in tongues. I realize this is an area of great controversy in the Body of Christ, but I have to mention it because it was instrumental in me overcoming depression. I believe the contention about tongues is due mostly to ignorance and the plan of the enemy to keep this awesome power hidden from God's children. First Corinthians 14:2 says when you pray in the spirit, (1) that you are praying directly to God, and (2) you are praying mysteries and secrets. This means that when you get born again, God's Spirit comes to live in you (John 14:16, 26, 16:13). The Holy Spirit, among many things, is our teacher and comforter; the language of the Spirit is tongues. As a believer, you are now afforded, through the Spirit of God, the benefit of speaking to God in a language He understands and a language encrypted and inaccessible to Satan. It is this continual praying in the spirit that gave me the revelation of how to get free from depression and is instrumental in unfolding these truths in this book.

Am I an expert on the subject of depression? No! But I sincerely believe God has given me a profound understanding that will pierce the heart of millions. So read on. As I peel off the layers of depression and you began to see clearly, the results are irrefutable. You will discover someone you never knew existed, and someone the world has been waiting for—THE REAL YOU.

Let's get on with it, what is depression?

Depression: A Worldly View   *2*

*I*n order to present a comprehensive, effective antithesis about depression, it is necessary that we understand the *world's* view because as the scripture says, "As a man thinketh in his heart, so is he" (Proverbs 23:7). If we embrace what the world says about depression, as statistics reveal we have, then we will accept and tolerate depression. You don't have to! Let's first expose what you may have been told about depression and then in the next chapter review extensively what the Kingdom of God has to say about it.

Depression Defined

The American Psychiatric Association defines depression as a serious medical illness or depressive disorder that negatively affects how you feel, think, or act. The National Institute of Mental Health (NIMH) defines a depressive disorder as an illness that involves the body, mood, and thoughts. It affects the way a person eats and sleeps, the way one feels about oneself, and the way one thinks about things. Overall, the consensus among clinicians and mental health professionals is that it is a disorder that affects the mind.

Contributing Factors

Many sources cite several predisposing factors as causes for depression, to include, chemical imbalances (changes in nerve pathways and brain chemicals called neurotransmitters that affect moods and thoughts); genetics (a biological vulnerability that can be inherited); personality (people with low self-esteem); and environmental factors (individuals who are predisposed to violence, abuse, and poverty—releasing a sense of hopelessness).

Victims

According to the NIMH, during a given year, approximately 1 in 10 adults will suffer from some form of depression (NIMH, 2006). They report that in any one-year period, 9.5 percent of the population, or about 18.8 million American adults, suffer from a depressive disorder. Depression, they purport, can strike anyone regardless of age, ethnic background, socioeconomic status or gender. One source disclosed some 41 actors and actresses, authors and writers, singers and musicians, and even businessmen and politicians who admitted their struggle with a depressive disorder, some ending in suicide. Those most noted were, Marilyn Monroe, Elvis Presley, Freddie Prinze, Sigmund Freud, Jimi Hendrix, Jim Belushi, Vincent Van Gogh and Ernest Hemingway; all or most of whom we all know and were well respected.

Other individuals at risk include those who are continuously exposed to violence, neglect, poverty, or abuse. In other words according to statistics, depression can affect anyone—even a person who appears to live in relatively ideal circumstances. The good news they assert, is that there is medical *treatment* for depression. However, not only is it costly, but often times unhealthy.

Treatment

Mental health professionals admit that there is no cure for depression. They are, however, pleased with the variety of drugs that have emerged to treat *the symptoms of* depression. Unfortunately, in every prescription, the list of side effects is troubling. Some of these include: nausea, vomiting, diarrhea or constipation, weight loss or gain, drowsiness, anxiety, insomnia, and headaches; more serious side effects include memory problems and poor concentration, sexual problems, bleeding problems, seizures and psychosis, rise in blood pressure, disturbance of heart rhythm, and kidney problems over time. Notwithstanding the cost for treating this ailment in America is reportedly over 40 billion dollars and the prognosis is recurrence especially in those with more than one episode.

After reading this, you may have two reactions: (1) who then can be helped and (2) why does a Christian need to know this? These questions are the very reason this information was included. Depression is very real. However, ***the strength of depression is one's belief about depression***. Proverbs 4:7 says, *"Wisdom is the principal thing; therefore get wisdom: and with all thy getting get understanding."*

In the court of law, when a case is presented, a good attorney will present enough facts that the jury can render a fair verdict. My goal is to present the truth so you can make a wise decision and be forever free. Since you live in this world you must know that you have been influenced by its subliminal messages. The media portrays depression as common and treatable, resulting in an increasing number of people accepting and taking medication to manage depression rather than eradicating it from their lives.

The truth is, undeniably, too many Christians are suffering from depression. In Luke 16, Jesus said that the children of this world are in their generation wiser than the children of light. Why? Because God's children have a system that provides amazing benefits; total life prosperity. However, either due to a lack of knowledge or sheer laziness, we do not take advantage of these benefits. This system is called the Kingdom of God and we are citizens of this kingdom. Let's thoroughly review the Kingdom of God and its response to depression so we can begin to enjoy an enviable life.

Citizens of the Kingdom 3

⊷≫ৡ৶⊶

*I*remember the first time I heard the term, "Kingdom of God." I immediately thought of the angels, Gabriel and Michael, and the twenty-four elders surrounding the throne of God with smoke permeating the air as they celebrated the presence of God—or something like that. Perhaps you did too. The Kingdom of God is not this at all.

> *"And leaving Nazareth, He went and dwelt in Capernaum by the sea, in the country of Zebulun and Naphtali—That what was spoken by the prophet Isaiah might be brought to pass: The land of Zebulun and the land of Naphtali, in the way to the sea, beyond the Jordan, Galilee of the Gentiles [of the peoples who are not of Israel]—The people who sat (dwelt enveloped) in darkness have seen a great Light, and for those who sat in the land and shadow of death Light has dawned. From that time Jesus began to preach, crying out, Repent (change your mind for the better, heartily amend your ways, with abhorrence of your past sins), for the kingdom of heaven is at hand" (Matthew 4:13-17, Amplified).*

This was Jesus' initial sermon or as some like to call it, His inaugural speech. He saw that the people were suffering from the pains of life. So, He began announcing that another system, the Kingdom of God, was available; not a system of this world that we would **depend on,** but a new system that would **unhook** us from every other system that was governing our lives; a system that was keeping us from the reality of God and His provisions and keeping us from the power of God being demonstrated in and through our lives.

Matthew 6:33 defines the Kingdom of God, or "this new system." It reads:

> *"But seek (aim at and strive after) first of all His kingdom and His righteousness (His way of doing and being right), and then all these things taken together will be given you besides" (Amplified).*

According to this scripture the Kingdom of God is the government of God; the realm of God; or simply put, God's way of doing things.

Colossians 1:12-13 says,

> *"Giving thanks to the Father, Who has qualified and made us fit to share the portion which is the inheritance of the saints (God's holy people) in the Light. [The Father] has delivered and drawn us to Himself out of the control and the dominion of darkness and has transferred us into the kingdom of the Son of His love" (Amplified).*

> *The New Living Translation (NLT) says:*

> *"For he has rescued us from the one who rules in the kingdom of darkness, and he has brought us into the kingdom of his dear son."*

This scripture reveals what happened when you became born again. Automatically, you were translated out of one system into another. You were snatched out of the clutches of Satan's Kingdom and given citizenship in the Kingdom of God. Certainly, we are not referring to the Kingdom of God as a geographical location like the Kingdom of Saudi Arabia or the United Kingdom. The Kingdom of God cannot be seen.

> *"And when he was demanded of the Pharisees, when the Kingdom of God should come, he answered them and said, The Kingdom of God cometh not with observation: Neither shall they say, Lo here! or, lo there! for, behold, the Kingdom of God is within you" (Luke 17:20-21).*

The Kingdom of God is a spiritual reality that cannot be comprehended with the natural mind. It is a spiritual term. We must understand the spirit realm, because it is the parent realm. Everything in the natural realm came out of the spirit realm (John 1:1-4).

This is not as strange as it may sound. All humans can perceive reality beyond the natural realm; the five senses — what you can see, touch, smell, hear, or taste. You already believe things you cannot see. For example, in the physical realm we know that there are germs that are microscopic. Under a microscope we've seen them or trust that somebody else has seen them. How do we know this? Because we wash our hands and we do other things to clean ourselves even though we don't see any germs because we've come to believe that there are things that exist that we don't see. Another example is radio and television signals. They are all around you right now even as you are reading this book, yet, you cannot see them. However, you can prove it by plugging in a radio or television set and turning it on. You can receive those signals and the broadcast.

So, we've come to realize that there are things that are there that we cannot see, touch, smell, hear, or taste. Well, that is just in the physical world. There is an entire spiritual world and spiritual realities that exist. The Kingdom of God is a spiritual reality. But you can't get it through your natural senses. Jesus told Nicodemus, *"Except a man be born again, he cannot see the Kingdom of God."* The word "see" here translates to "perceive and understand." As a believer, you have a right to understand the mysteries of the Kingdom of God (Matthew13:11).

In one of the most profound teachings I've heard on the Kingdom of God, Dr. Myles Munroe states that every Kingdom must have:

(1) A King
(2) Territory
(3) Citizens
(4) Constitution
(5) Laws
(6) Government
(7) Privileges
(8) Code of ethics
(9) Great Influence

As believers, we are citizens of the Kingdom of God and our kingdom is ruled by God. What is His plan for this kingdom? "... Thy will be done in earth, as it is in heaven" (Matthew 6:10).There is no sickness in heaven; no bad marriages in heaven; no poverty in heaven; no depression in heaven. We are supposed to have days of heaven right here on earth (Deuteronomy 11:21).

When God delivered us out of the kingdom of darkness which is ruled by Satan and transferred us into the Kingdom of God, He became our King and He established a new set of standards by which we can live. We now live under the government of God, no longer governed by that old system with its limitations and destruction. We simply must learn how to operate the principles governing this Kingdom. (Two excellent resources on this subject are: "Rediscovering the Kingdom," by Dr. Myles Munroe [www.bfmmm.com] and "The Kingdom of God in You," by Dr. Bill Winston [www.bwm.org]).

A Note on Carnal-Mindedness

As a believer, you are in covenant with God and must not think like a naturally minded (or carnal) person if you are to appropriate the zoe life of God.

"This I say therefore, and testify in the Lord, that ye henceforth walk not as other Gentiles walk, in the vanity of their mind" (*Ephesians 4:17*).

The word *Gentile* is talking about a person not in covenant with God. The vernacular we would use today is not to walk like a lost man, one who doesn't have a relationship with God. How do they walk, in the vanity of their minds. In other words, don't let your mind be controlled by carnal physical things, but instead use that mind and renew it.

Another scripture is Romans 8:6, *"For to be carnally minded is death; but to be spiritually minded is life and peace."*

Carnal mindedness doesn't necessarily mean sinful mindedness. The word *carnal* literally means of the five senses. In other words, don't let your mind be dominated only by what it can see, touch, smell, taste or feel. If you don't start thinking spiritually instead of carnally, then you will shut off the flow of the life of God through you. This scripture correlates carnally minded with being fleshly minded which is death. But the rest of the verse says to be spiritual minded is life and peace. The mathematical equation would read, spiritually mindedness = life and peace; carnal mindedness = death. This isn't talking about only physical death but depression is death, emotional distress is death. Carnal mindedness produces death. John 6:63 defines spiritual mindedness, *"the words I speak unto you they are spirit and they are life."* So, spiritual mindedness means Word-mindedness. If you are dominated more by what God's Word has to say than by what your five senses say, then all you will produce is life and peace.

Now that we have some understanding of the Kingdom of God, we are ready for the kingdom response to the worldly view of depression.

The Kingdom Response

Let me begin this discussion by stating that the following information is not presented to minimize the power of depression; it is a powerful foe. My intent, however, is to offer you hope that you can overcome depression, not just manage it. However, it will require faith and for some a significant paradigm shift which this book will help you achieve. The message of the Kingdom is that you can overcome the pressures of this world. It simply requires changing your mentality to operate by another system, the Kingdom of God System. Let's review the four variables introduced in the previous chapter: *Clinical Definition, Contributing Factors, Chemical Imbalances, and Genetics and Environment.*

Clinical Definition

In the previous chapter depression was defined as a medical illness or depressive disorder that negatively affects how you feel, think or act. The consensus is that it is a disorder that affects the mind. What does the Kingdom of God say about the mind? 1 Peter 5:8 tells us "to be of sober mind," which suggests if I gain control of my thoughts, I will not be prey to the enemy which uses depression to oppress me. Luke 10:19 also says, *"Behold! I have given you authority and power to trample upon serpents and scorpions, and [physical and **mental strength** and ability] over all the power that the enemy [possesses]; and nothing shall in any way harm you"* *(Amplified).* This is such an important topic that I have dedicated an entire chapter on the mind, so we'll leave this for the moment.

Contributing Factors

Three of the predisposing factors for depression included:
1. Chemical imbalances
2. Genetics
3. Environmental factors

Chemical Imbalances

Depression, researchers assert, is somehow linked to a chemical imbalance. Careful research on this topic, however, reveals that not even doctors, scientists or clinical researchers know exactly what causes a chemical imbalance. Interestingly, over the years, researchers have noted a handful of possible underlying reasons to include the theory that chemical imbalance actually stems from our own thoughts and actions. You're probably asking like I did, "How does one's own thoughts and behaviors affect the balance of brain chemicals?" I'm not a scientist, but after reviewing the material, it is really not difficult to understand. Let me attempt to explain it in layman terms.

Think about what happens when you avoid an accident or when you see a police car over a hill after you've been speeding. You've guessed it, that adrenalin is pumping. Our brain is designed to process incoming information and create a response. All of these processes happen extremely quickly in the brain, causing a chemical imbalance. The effects of a chemical imbalance may lead to undue stress, nervousness and worry — depression.

To some extent, the Bible supports this theory. Consider Proverbs 14:30, "*A calm and undisturbed mind and heart are the life and health of the body, but envy, jealousy, and wrath are like rottenness of the bones.*" Proverbs 17:22, says, "*A happy heart is good medicine and **a cheerful mind works healing**, but a broken spirit dries up the bones.*" The solution from a kingdom perspective: stay out of stress.

Genetics & Environment

The most common argument about depression is that it is genetic, i.e., it runs in the family. If Big Mama had it, you'll probably develop it; if Uncle Nestor had it, chances are you'll have it. While I agree that there may be some dysfunctional patterns, for example alcoholism and abuse throughout one's family, an alternative perspective is that this is not necessarily genetics, but the manifestation of familiar spirits.

Most believers are unaware these spirits exist. The Authorized Version (King James) uses the term "familiar spirit" sixteen times. What are familiar spirits? This term refers to a spirit of divination, or to its medium (Leviticus 20:27; Deuteronomy 18:11; Acts 16:16). A parallel term in the Hebrew means "to know, a knowing spirit, one who is made wise by contacting the nether world." It is a spirit that is familiar with a person, a place, or a thing. Literally, it is used to describe the spirit belonging to the family and therefore knows things about the members of that family. In other words, it is a spirit that is familiar with you because it has been around you since you were born.

One of the most descriptive accounts in the Old Testament is in 1 Samuel 28, when Saul sought the counsel of a witch to try to contact Samuel who was dead. The "Witch of Endor" expected to call up the spirit she was familiar with—her control spirit. Then when Samuel appeared instead of her familiar control spirit, she was surprised and frightened and it was only then that she recognized Saul as King.

So familiar spirits have knowledge about you because they have been around you and your family for generations. They are familiar with you and will communicate this information to other spirits.

This may help explain how alcoholism, abuse, sexual perversion, drug addiction, depression, etc. is seen prevalent in families. These *spirits* of alcoholism, sexual perversion, or depression have been around the family for generations. Spirits that are familiar with you have watched your every move and waited for the opportunity to manifest in your life.

Spousal abuse is an excellent example. Statistics report that children who witness violence against their mothers are likely to become victims later on in life or themselves become offenders. This is not because these individuals carry a gene that causes physical aggression or compliance, but because of menacing familiar spirits.

So, if someone in your family suffers from or is haunted by depression, that doesn't mean you are a *carrier* of a "depression gene," it may simply denote the presence of a familiar spirit that is attempting to thwart the plan of God for your life as it has all those who walk in ignorance. Rest assured their primary goal is to "kill, steal, and destroy:" (John 10:10). Thank God for 2 Corinthians 2:14, *"Now thanks be unto God, which always causeth us to triumph in Christ..."* As a believer, purchased by the precious blood of Jesus, you have the authority to break every generational curse in your life.

> *"Christ has redeemed us from the curse of the law, having become a curse for us (for it is written, 'Cursed is everyone who hangs on a tree') ..." [Galatians 3:13].*
> *"...God was in Christ reconciling the world to Himself, not imputing their trespasses to them..."(2 Corinthians 5:19).*
> *"...For I will forgive their iniquity, and their sin I will remember no more" (Jeremiah 31:34).*

You can get free from this now by praying this prayer and releasing your faith so that you can receive deliverance for you and your family:

Prayer

Father, I thank you that Jesus has redeemed me from the curse. I believe that according to your Word, you have forgiven my sins and do not count them against me. I accept your forgiveness and acknowledge that Jesus has taken away my sin and the sin of my family. I thank you that every generational curse is broken in my family, in the name of Jesus.

Genetics or Fleshly Behavior?

Lastly, believers have used the argument of genetics or heredity as an excuse to justify many of their fleshy behavior, such as "I'm mean because I have my mother's temper." The problem with such deception, and this is deception, is if Satan can convince you to accept this untruth, he can get you to accept other beguiling information such as piety is directly proportionate to poverty, or God puts a sickness on you to teach you something. We must make the Word of God the final authority in our lives and govern all of our decisions, actions and habits based on its authenticity.

"Therefore if any person is [ingrafted] in Christ (the Messiah) he is a new creation (a new creature altogether); the old [previous moral and spiritual condition] has passed away. Behold, the fresh and new has come!"(2 Corinthians 5:17).

Who is At Risk and Treatment?

The statistics presented on the number of adults that will suffer from depression in a given year are staggering and unacceptable. Sadly, reports indicate that pre-schoolers are the fastest-growing market for antidepressants. At least four percent of preschoolers—over a million—are clinically depressed (NIMH, 2007). This is disheartening. This book is dedicated to providing you with information that will eradicate depression from you and your family's life permanently.

Prescription medication has been the main course of treatment for depressive disorders. Prescription drugs, however, have failed to be the silver bullet that the drug manufacturers have hoped they would be. Moreover, as discussed, with every prescription there is also a lengthy list of harmful side effects and consequences once treatment using these drugs has stopped. Some literature suggests that the commonly prescribed selective serotonin reuptake inhibitors

(SSRIs) might increase suicidal thinking in some people, particularly children. The Federal Drug Administration Panel (May, 2007) has directed pharmaceutical companies to label these drugs to indicate these negative effects, to include warnings to young adults and even older patients.

In recent years, the aggressive advertising of drugs directly to consumers has also boosted demand for antidepressants. The amount the pharmaceutical industry spent on television and print advertisements aimed at the public grew exponentially during the new millennium. In 2000, consumer advertising increased 31.5 percent. The pharmaceutical producers spent $2.8 billion in 2001 on consumer advertising—an increase of 12 percent. The result: overall, Americans paid about $208 billion in 2001 for prescription drugs— almost double that spent in 1996. More than seven million people took an antidepressant in 2001—up 700,000 from 2000. Statistics for more current years are pending but promises to be alarmingly high. While these pharmaceutical companies are benefiting immensely from these treatment options, government reporting indicates that 70 percent of people with depression continue to have unresolved symptoms throughout their lifetime.

Recently I was asked whether Christians should take medication for depression and at this point you may be pondering the same thought. I am not opposing doctors or medicine. I am simply saying don't depend on doctors or medicine alone to keep you healthy. There are some diseases that medical science cannot cure. But, if you need a doctor, see a doctor. Many lives are saved every year through medical assistance. If a believer is traumatized by depression and is in harm's way, i.e., severely dysfunctional, nonfunctional, or suicidal, my response is unequivocally yes; by all means take whatever medication the physician prescribes, but mix faith with it by saying, "I believe I receive my healing and will experience no harmful side effects from taking these meds, in Jesus' Name." This is true also for taking medication for any life-threatening disease. I believe emphatically that the Word of God answers all; that it provides the cardinal remedy for every problem under the sun, but it works by faith and faith does not come until your mind is renewed. This takes time. If a person is seriously ill whether physically or mentally, the Word of God may not have adequate time to work. Therefore, take the meds until you are out of danger, then start a regimen of renewing your mind with the Word of God. Don't stop taking the medication until the Lord has directed you to do so.

God knows how to take care of His children. His awesome plan provides for your well-being. He doesn't want you walking around with poor concentration or blurred vision; that makes you open prey for the adversary. What would stop you from getting hit or run over by a Mack truck? What about sexual intimacy? As covenant partners your intimacy should be dripping with the anointing; the marriage bed is undefiled (Hebrews 13:4). Yet, because of adverse side-effects of some of these drugs, your desire for your mate has all but waned. This opens the door once again to the adversary against your marriage, family, and can alter the course of your life.

Closing Argument

In the Kingdom there are benefits:

"BLESS (AFFECTIONATELY, gratefully praise) the Lord, O my soul; and all that is [deepest] within me, bless His holy name! Bless (affectionately, gratefully praise) the Lord, O my soul, and forget not [one of] all His benefits—Who

forgives [every one of] all your iniquities, Who heals [each one of] all your diseases, Who redeems your life from the pit and corruption, Who beautifies, dignifies, and crowns you with loving-kindness and tender mercy; Who satisfies your mouth [your necessity and desire at your personal age and situation] with good so that your youth, renewed, is like the eagle's [strong, overcoming, soaring]!" (Psalms 103:1-5, Amplified).

Note that included in this list of fringe benefits is that He heals all your diseases. According to medical science, depression is a disease.

First Peter 1:23 says, *"You have been regenerated (born again) not from a mortal origin (seed, sperm) but from one that is immortal by the ever living and lasting Word of God" (Amplified).* The Authorized Version says *"we are born again not of corruptible seed, but of incorruptible, by the Word of God..."* That means if we are born by the Word of God, then we must be sustained by the Word of God. In other words, the Word of God provides the only solution for our lives. The Word [itself] testifies of this:

> *"Then they cry unto the LORD in their trouble, and he saveth them out of their distresses. He sent **his Word**, and healed them, and delivered them from their destructions"* (Psalms 107:19-20).
> *"My son, attend to **my words**; consent and submit to my sayings. Let them not depart from your sight; keep them in the center of your heart. For they are life to those who find them, healing and health to all their flesh" (Proverbs 4:20-22).*

In the preceding chapter the prognosis for depression is at best bleak. But the prognosis for depression from a kingdom perspective is a 100 percent cure rate for those who believe and act on the truths revealed in this book. The layers we have peeled away thus far reveal that many suffer from depression either because of (1) embracing the world's way of thinking about depression or (2) ignorance of the benefits offered in the Kingdom of God. Understanding how your mind has been programmed by the world is pivotal in removing yet another layer of depression. Let's explore this in the next chapter.

The Tripartite Nature of Man 4

⤠

*A*n article printed in the Christian Counselor stated, *"If I were asked if there is one subject that I deal with more than others in counseling, I would say it is depression. It has reached epidemic proportions in our society today. Many people wonder why. Christians sometimes wrongly think they are immune to its dark clutches. Yet, many Christians deal with depression daily."*

The Composition of Man

When sharing my testimony about depression, I was often asked how this was possible since I was a Christian. The answer is quite simple. Christians represent a microcosm of the world. When you become born again, your thinking, which is instrumental in your well being, doesn't automatically change. In other words, there is not an immediate transformation of the human soul. Recall the Apostle John says, *"Beloved, I wish above all things that thou mayest prosper and be in health, even as thou soul prospereth"* (3 John 2). He is correlating your wholeness with the prosperity of your soul. First Thessalonians 5:23 defines the tripartite nature of man as spirit, soul, and body.

"And may the God of peace Himself sanctify you through and through [separate you from profane things, make you pure and wholly consecrated to God]; and may your spirit and soul and body be preserved sound and complete [and found] blameless at the coming of our Lord Jesus Christ (the Messiah)" (Amplified).

This scripture reveals that man is spirit, has a soul and lives in a body. As a Christian, your spirit is just like God, perfect (John 4:24, Gen 1:26). It is your spirit that communes with God. Your soul (mind, will, and emotions) on the other hand, remains in the same condition it was before you were saved and is in desperate need of a major overhaul. Nothing, absolutely nothing happened to your soul when you became born again.

Second Corinthians 5:17 says Christians are new creatures, but this verse is simply talking about your spiritual condition or your stance with God. Because of Adam's sin man was separated from God, but because of Jesus' obedience man has been reconciled back to God. When a person is born again, he is brought back into harmony with God and has the ability to communicate with Him and to cultivate the zoe life. The Scripture says, "How can two walk together except they agree?" (Amos 3:3). It is paramount that you understand the place of the soul. When you become born again, nothing changes but your spirit. In the natural, you are still married to the same person; still faced with the same discouraging circumstances, same facts, etc. You look for all the changes to take place in the physical realm, but it is a process; only your spirit changes instantly, not your soul or way of thinking.

Here is an example I often use to explain this truth. Let's say, before you became born again you knew absolutely nothing about Physics. The next day after your conversion, you are not handpicked to sit on a panel at the Massachusetts Institute of Technology, School of Science. Why? Because there was no physical change, only a spiritual one. Likewise, if you were overweight the day you went to the altar and gave your life to Christ, when you returned to your seat you could not shout with jubilant joy because miraculously you can now walk the runway with Heidi Klum or Tyra Banks or for you guys, replace Taye Diggs or Patrick Dempsey as America's heart-throb. This is, of course, irrational. Why, because nothing happened to you physically, only spiritually.

The Taming of the Soul

What we fail to realize is that our soul is in desperate need of conversion. It was not only trained by the world (our experiences and environment, for example), but in its flawed state, continues to wrestle for control. It insists on its own way.

> *"So get rid of all uncleanness and the rampant outgrowth of wickedness, and in a humble (gentle, modest) spirit receive and welcome the Word which implanted and rooted [in your hearts] contains the power to save your souls" (James 1:21).*
>
> *"The law of the LORD is perfect, converting the soul: the testimony of the LORD is sure, making wise the simple" (Psalms 19:7).*

Jesus, Himself, revealed the seriousness of dealing with your corrupt soul—and this is something **you** must do. In other words, Christ, through redemption, took care of the spirit of man; He left the discipline and conversion of the soul to the individual.

> *"By **your** steadfastness and patient endurance you shall win the true life of your souls" (Luke 21:19, Amplified).*

43

How the Soul Was Trained

Your thinking (mind) has been shaped by, or patterned after, the world. And what you *picked up* and therefore did while you were in the "world" does not immediately change. Proverbs 22:6 says *"Train up a child in the way he should go: and when he is old, he will not depart from it."* That means your "way of thinking" is potentially permanent until you receive new information.

Ignorantly, this is the very thing I neglected to do. Although I gave my heart to the Lord, I did nothing to convert my soul; which simply consisted of renewing my mind with the Word of God. Of course, it wasn't until years later that I even knew such conversion was necessary. That's why it is important where you attend church. You must sit under an anointed man or woman of God who **"knows and teaches the truth."** You will not get free from *any* oppression until you do. We are in this world and must recognize and, on purpose, attack any thinking that does not line up with the Word of God. Unfortunately many believers are ignorant of this implication so let's spend some time explaining the "world system."

The Truth about the World System

For purposes of this book, when referring to the "world" we are not using this synonymously with the word "earth." The Vine's Expository Dictionary of Biblical Words defines *world* in the Greek as, *aion,* denoting an age, a period of time; the force attaching to the word is not so much that of the actual length of a period, but that of a period marked by spiritual or moral characteristics. Romans 12:2 will assist us immensely in our attempt to fully disclose its meaning.

"I APPEAL to you therefore, brethren, and beg of you in view of [all] the mercies of God, to make a decisive dedication of your bodies [presenting all your members and faculties] as a living sacrifice, holy (devoted, consecrated) and well pleasing to God, which is your reasonable (rational, intelligent) service and spiritual worship. Do not be conformed to this world (this age), [fashioned after and adapted to its external, superficial customs], but be transformed (changed) by the [entire] renewal of your mind [by its new ideals and its new attitude], so that you may prove [for yourselves] what is the good and acceptable and perfect will of God, even the thing which is good and acceptable and perfect [in His sight for you]" (Romans 12:1-2, Amplified).

Consider the New Living Translation of this same scripture:

"And so, dear brothers and sisters, I plead with you to give your bodies to God. Let them be a living and holy sacrifice — the kind he will accept. When you think of what he has done for you, is this too much to ask? Don't copy the behavior and customs of this world, but let God transform you into a new person by changing the way you think. Then you will know what God wants you to do, and you will know how good and pleasing and perfect his will really is."

This is one of the most powerful scriptures in the Bible for believers seriously wanting to appropriate the God kind of life. The Apostle Paul is begging, pleading with believers concerning our relationship with God. This alone warrants our attention. He begs us to live holy (the literal translation denoting being at one mind with God) and then warns us not to conform or ***pattern ourselves*** after the customs or traditions of this world.

The word *conformed* means to be formed into the mold of something. In other words, there is pressure from the world, the devil, unbelievers, and circumstances for you to accept defeat, failure, hurt and, for example, depression. You are being pressed by these afflictions, but you don't have to fit into that mold. Eventually, the pressure will melt you. Even as a believer, you can't go through life without being pressured; one way or the other, you will be changed. You will be melted, but you get to pick what mold you fit into; the one that God says about you or what the world says about you. You don't have to become bitter or experience the defeat that the world offers you. You are going to change but you get to pick what kind of change that is; whether it is a metamorphosis into something better or plunging into something worse.

The word *transformed* in the Greek is *metamorphoo*, the word we get metamorphosis from; the process **where a little worm spins a cocoon and turns into a butterfly**. If you want that kind of change, changing from the depressive person to the victorious person, Romans 12:2 says it is by the renewing of your mind. What you think in your mind determines whether you experience the life of God or the death and defeat of the natural realm and it is the renewing of your mind that changes all that.

So, what the Apostle Paul is intimating is that while we were in the world, separated from God, we developed a mindset contrary to the mind of God. Consequently, every believer **must** renew his mind. How do you renew your mind? It is through the Word of God that you renew your mind. The Word tells you what is *spiritually* true. It gives you new values and you must change your mind to these values. As a believer, you must furnish your mind with new information; information resembling the life of God so you can prove for yourself His perfect will for you; total life prosperity. Another way of saying this is your mind must be re-programmed. Why? Because while you were in the world—separated from God—you developed a mindset contrary to the mind of God and the only solution is to have your mind renewed—and this is something you must do.

Let's examine other scriptures that further explain this concept of what was happening to us while we were in the world.

> *"And you hath he quickened, who were dead in trespasses and sins; Wherein in time past ye walked according to the course of this world, according to the prince of the power of the air, the spirit that now worketh in the children of disobedience: Among whom also we all had our conversation in times past in the lusts of our flesh, fulfilling the desires of the flesh and of the mind; and were by nature the children of wrath, even as others" (Ephesians 2:1-3).*

Note the Amplified Version:

> *"AND YOU [He made alive], when you were dead (slain) by [your] trespasses and sins In which at one time you walked [habitually]. You were following the course and fashion of this world [were under the sway of the tendency of this present age], following the prince of the power of the air. [You were obedient to and under the control of] the [demon] spirit that still constantly works in the sons of disobedience [the careless, the rebellious, and the unbelieving, who go against the purposes of God]. Among these we as well as you once lived and conducted ourselves in the passions of our flesh [our behavior governed by our corrupt and sensual nature], obeying the impulses of the flesh and the thoughts of the mind [our cravings dictated by our senses and our dark imaginings]. We were then by nature children of [God's] wrath and heirs of [His] indignation, like the rest of mankind."*

The literal translation of *world* in Ephesians 2:1 is interestingly, the word *aion*, "age," and the word *kosmos*, "world," which together translates, "the age of this world-system." So, the Apostle is confirming that before we got born again we were influenced, trained and programmed by the prince of the air. Who is the prince of the air? Satan, of course. Similar titles are found elsewhere in the Scripture concerning Satan. Satan is called the "god of this world" in 2 Corinthians 4:4. He is called the "ruler of this world" in John 12:31. These titles, and many more ascribed to Satan throughout the Scripture, convey his capabilities. To say, for example, that Satan is the "prince of the power of the air" is to convey that in some way he rules over the world and the people therein. Believers, however, are no longer under the rule of Satan (Colossians 1:13). Unbelievers, and unbelieving believers, on the other hand, are caught "in the snare of the devil" (2 Timothy 2:26), lie in the "power of the evil one" (1 John 5:19), and are in bondage to Satan (Ephesians 2:2), simply because they fail to renew their minds to the truth found in the Word of God.

Let me provide an example in the Old Testament that will assist us in understanding how one can be programmed and influenced by the world. In the Old Testament, we know that the children of Israel were in bondage in Egypt for over 400 years (Genesis 15:13, Exodus 12:40). Egypt is, of course, a type of the world. Although a people marked by God, and for God, while under the rulership of Pharaoh (a type of Satan), they learned the customs of these Gentile people that ultimately kept them from believing God (Psalm 78:41). How do we know this?

"WHEN THE people saw that Moses delayed to come down from the mountain, [they] gathered together to Aaron, and said to him, Up, make us gods to go before us; as for this Moses, the man who brought us up out of the land of Egypt,

we do not know what has become of him. So Aaron replied, Take the gold rings from the ears of your wives, your sons, and daughters, and bring them to me. So all the people took the gold rings from their ears and brought them to Aaron. And he received the gold at their hand and fashioned it with a graving tool and made it a molten calf; and they said, These are your gods, O Israel, which brought you up out of the land of Egypt! And when Aaron saw the molten calf, he built an altar before it; and Aaron made proclamation, and said, Tomorrow shall be a feast to the Lord" (Exodus 32:1-5).

Why did they make gods? This is the image that was in their hearts. Where did they learn this? They learned it while they were in Egypt (Exodus 12:2; 15:11, 20:3). When the pressure was on, they reverted back to what they knew—what they had learned when in Egypt; the world.

Likewise, unless you have intentionally renewed your mind to the Word of God, you have developed a mindset that is in desperate need of a paradigm shift. What was Satan's strategy? He programmed our minds with our environments using education, our neighborhoods, media, images, people, influences, relatives, experiences, exposures, television, etc. He used basically the same principle that Jesus taught in Matthew's Gospel, *the sower sowed the Word.*

"Another parable put he forth unto them, saying, The kingdom of heaven is likened unto a man which sowed good seed in his field: But while men slept, his enemy came and sowed tares among the wheat, and went his way. But when the blade was sprung up, and brought forth fruit, then appeared the tares also. So the servants of the householder came and said unto him, Sir, didst not thou sow good seed in thy field? from whence then hath it tares? He said unto them, An enemy hath done this. The servants said unto him, Wilt thou then that we go and gather them up?" (Matthew 13:24-28)

Satan sowed something but it wasn't the Word. He sowed lies and the result was those things coming into our minds establishing a mental block that we are not healed, that we are not blessed, that we cannot live the abundant life. This is why Jesus said be not of this world.

> *"I have given them your word. And the world hates them because they do not belong to the world, just as I do not. I'm not asking you to take them out of the world, but to keep them safe from the evil one. They are not part of this world any more than I am. Make them pure and holy by teaching them your words of truth. As you sent me into the world, I am sending them into the world. And I give myself entirely to you so they also might be entirely yours" (John 17:14-19, NLT).*

What did our Lord and Savior mean in this dialog? Is this language admonishing us to separate ourselves from this world? Of course not, we are the world's only hope; the world is our harvest (John 3:16-18, Romans 8:19). We are not to separate ourselves as if to convey some sense of superiority, but rather separate ourselves through the way we think so we can prove the perfect will of God for all mankind. John 17:17 says, *"Sanctify them [purify, consecrate, separate them for Yourself, make them holy] by the Truth; Your Word is Truth" (Amplified).*

In other words, Jesus is praying to the Father to set us apart by the Word of God. The Word of God will separate us from the world and the world's system; the world's way of thinking (doing and being wrong).

Satan's only hope is to keep you from the truth and although we have what my husband calls "perfect church attendance," there is no metamorphosis of the soul, and until the soul has been changed by the engrafted Word of God, we will continue to experience these roller coaster rides in our minds, without ever leaving our homes.

If depression is a curse and the Word says, "Christ has redeemed us from the curse of the law being made a curse for us" (Galatians 3:13), why then are there proportionally as many Christians suffering from depression as non-Christians? Because we are either not hearing the truth or not acting on what we hear. The Word of God is the perfect law of liberty.

"But he who looks carefully into the faultless law, the [law] of liberty, and is faithful to it and perseveres in looking into it, being not a heedless listener who forgets but an active doer [who obeys], he shall be blessed in his doing (his life of obedience)" (James 1:25, Amplified).

When we look into the mirror, we make whatever changes the mirror exposes. This is the analogy the Apostle is using. The Word of God is the perfect law of liberty. It liberates; it emancipates from slavery. But if we fail to give attention to the Word of God (look into it but fail to correct whatever flaw it reveals) it will profit us nothing—as powerful as it is—it will not profit you at all. We've almost reached the core but have a few more layers to uncover, let's continue.

What's in Your Spirit? 5

*I*think we are now ready to fully grasp the truth about depression. Like leprosy is a disease of the physical body, depression is a disease of the soul. It is the result of not taming the soul (your mind, will and emotions). It is the result of the unyielding soul attempting to fight battles it is unequipped to win. Believers suffer with depression because too much attention is given to feelings and not enough to the Word of God.

The Empty Spirit Syndrome

As born again believers, we must understand what it takes to sustain us.

> *"God said, Let Us [Father, Son, and Holy Spirit] make mankind in Our image, after Our likeness, and let them have complete authority over the fish of the sea, the birds of the air, the [tame] beasts, and over all of the earth, and over everything that creeps upon the earth" (Genesis 1:26, Amplified).*
>
> *"God is a Spirit (a spiritual Being) and those who worship Him must worship Him in spirit and in truth (reality)" (John 4:24, Amplified).*

We are made in the image of God. Image here denotes sharing the inner attributes that breaks one down.

As we discussed previously, man is a tripartite being; spirit, soul and body. It is in our spirit that we share all the attributes that make God, God. That means that one third of us is absolutely like God. Our spirit is that part of us that is already completely changed. However, we must understand that no matter how perfect our spirit is, it must be sustained by the Word of God. Why? Everything that was made was made by the Word of God.

> *"Who being the brightness of his glory, and the express image of his person, and **upholding all things by the Word of his power,** when he had by himself purged our sins, sat down on the right hand of the Majesty on high" (Hebrews 1:3).*
>
> *"And to make all men see what is the fellowship of the mystery, which from the beginning of the world hath been hid in God, who created all things by Jesus Christ" (Ephesians 3:9).*
>
> *"IN THE beginning [before all time] was the Word (Christ), and the Word was with God, and the Word was God Himself. He was present originally with God. **All things were made and came into existence through Him (the Word);** and without Him was not even one thing made that has come into being" (John 1:1-3, Amplified).*

Jesus said it this way:

> *"But He replied, It has been written, Man shall not live and be upheld and sustained by bread alone, but by every word that comes forth from the mouth of God" (Matthew 4:4).*

Everything that was made (including you and I) was made by the Word of God. Since we were made by the Word of God, it is reasonable to conclude that the Word of God is the only means to sustain us. This revelation is severely underestimated in the church today. Every believer must have a daily supply of the Word of God. It is the fuel on which we are designed to operate. Now, I am speaking spiritual things. You must become convinced that without the Word of God in your heart you will never harvest the life of God and will always be prone to the tricks and strategies of the enemy, and equally important, your self-ruling soul.

> *"For even though by this time you ought to be teaching others, you actually need someone to teach you over again the very first principles of God's Word. You have come to need milk, not solid food" (Hebrews 5:12, Amplified).*

You may have been saved for a very long time. Yet, while you should be teaching others how to defeat depression, you have need for someone to teach you. Why, because you have allowed your spirit to become empty. You do not have enough Word in your spirit. Yes, you attend church regularly; perhaps you are in a leadership position. Feeding your spirit is not commensurate with church attendance; spiritual growth is not commensurate with church activity. You can join or head every department in your church, but if you are not getting a daily supply of the Word of God, you are (1) carnal and (2) a candidate for not only depression but all the oppressions of the enemy.

We must continuously measure our spiritual growth. I like to use this example. I can measure my granddaughter's chronological age not only by how tall she is growing, some kids grow faster or slower than others, but by how she is maturing. She is almost ten years old. If she was still wearing pampers or speaking baby talk, I would know we have a problem.

We measure our growth on our places of deployment (what others call employment) by our promotions, our educational level or number of degrees, etc. Yet, we fail to measure the most important part of us, our spiritual growth. How do we grow? We grow by the Word of God.

Rom 1:16 says:

> *"For I am not ashamed of the Gospel (good news) of Christ, for it is God's power working unto salvation [for deliverance from eternal death] to everyone who believes with a personal trust and a confident surrender and firm reliance, to the Jew first and also to the Greek" (Amplified).*
>
> *"As newborn babes, desire the sincere milk of the Word that you may grow thereby" (1 Peter 2:2).*

The Amplified Version says,

> *"Like newborn babies you should crave (thirst for, earnestly desire) the pure (unadulterated) spiritual milk, that by it you may be nurtured and grow unto [completed] salvation..."*

Don't be misled by the term newborn babes. Remember, you can't eat strong meat without first drinking milk. Milk is defined in the Authorized Version as the Word of God. We must understand that we need this milk ever flowing in our lives because it is the only way we can grow; notice the proportion to which we can grow, "to completed salvation." Both scriptures reveal that the Word of God brings *salvation*. This is a powerful term.

Salvation here in the Greek is *soteria*. It means soundness, wholeness, healing, prosperity, and preservation. In a nutshell, the Hebrew word *shalom*—nothing missing, nothing broken; nothing needed, nothing wanted. That means as believers, if we can get enough of the Word in our spirits, we can cultivate the God kind of life, free from stress, anxiety, lack, sickness, you name it.

Salvation then, is not just the new birth. Unfortunately, many believers are stuck in the new birth experience. They get born again, but never reach completed salvation. The new birth gets you into the Kingdom of God, completed salvation gets you the keys to the Kingdom of God—it allows you to operate just like God. Let's add additional scriptures to our scriptural repository:

> *"And now [brethren], I commit you to God [I deposit you in His charge, entrusting you to His protection and care]. And I commend you to the Word of His grace [to the commands and counsels and promises of His unmerited favor]. It is able to build you up and to give you [your rightful] inheritance among all God's set-apart ones (those consecrated, purified, and transformed of soul)" (Acts 20:32, Amplified).*

> *"And we also [especially] thank God continually for this, that when you received the message of God [which you heard] from us, you welcomed it not as the Word of [mere] men, but as it truly is, the Word of God, which is effectually at work in you who believe [exercising its superhuman power in those who adhere to and trust in and rely on it]" (1 Thessalonians 2:13, Amplified).*

> *"For the Word that God speaks is alive and full of power [making it active, operative, energizing, and effective]; it is sharper than any two-edged sword, penetrating to the dividing line of the breath of life (soul) and [the immortal] spirit, and of joints and marrow [of the deepest parts of our nature], exposing and sifting and analyzing and judging the very thoughts and purposes of the heart" (Hebrews 4:12, Amplified).*

> *"It is the spirit that quickeneth; the flesh profiteth nothing: the Words that I speak unto you, they are spirit, and they are life" (John 6:63).*

These are powerful scriptures revealing the power found in the Word of God. Finally, Jesus said the Word of God is spirit (*pneuma*) meaning alive and it provides (*zoe*), the God kind of life.

How Does the Word Get Into Your Spirit?

"And he said unto them, Unto you it is given to know the mystery of the Kingdom of God: but unto them that are without, all these things are done in parables: That seeing they may see, and not perceive; and hearing they may hear, and not understand; lest at any time they should be converted, and their sins should be forgiven them. And he said unto them, Know ye not this parable? and how then will ye know all parables? The sower soweth the word. And these are they by the way side, where the word is sown; but when they have heard, Satan cometh immediately, and taketh away the word that was sown in their hearts. And these are they like-wise which are sown on stony ground; who, when they have heard the word, immediately receive it with gladness; And have no root in themselves, and so endure but for a time: afterward, when affliction or persecution ariseth for the word's sake, immediately they are offended. And these are they which are sown among thorns; such as hear the word, And the cares of this world, and the deceitfulness of riches, and the lusts of other things entering in, choke the word, and it becometh unfruitful. And these are they which are sown on good ground; such as hear the word, and receive it, and bring forth fruit, some thirtyfold, some sixty, and some an hundred" (Mark 4:11-20).

God is always sowing the Word. He says however, that not everyone is hearing it. If you are not hearing the Word, it will never be conceived in your heart. This is why you can have one hundred members attending the same church and hearing the same Word, but see the Word manifested in different proportions in their lives;

some none, some thirty, some sixty, and some a hundredfold. Why, because they are not really *hearing* the Word. The standard you can use to discern whether you are hearing the Word is whether you are *doing* the Word. In other words, there must be comprehension to the point of application. Jesus said if you understand this parable, you can understand them all. At the moment you hear, see, or understand the Word, you can be converted into the Word, you see hear or understand (Matthew 13:15; Mark 4:12). For example, you can hear 1 Peter 2:24 for years (*"Who his own self bare our sins in his own body on the tree that we, being dead to sins, should live unto righteousness: by whose stripes ye were healed"*). According to this scripture, healing has been provided to every believer; yet, as many believers are dying to sickness as non-believers. Why? There is no redemptive revelation of this scripture in their hearts; conception has not taken place. No matter how many times a woman is intimate with her husband, she will not have a child until conception takes place. And it is rare that conception takes place the first time they are intimate.

Likewise, you must understand that Jesus is always sowing the Word, but distractions intentionally arise to keep you from becoming pregnant with the Word (Matthew 13:19; Mark 4:17; Luke 8:12). If you persevere through these distractions (Mark 4:17-19), you are guaranteed a harvest.

According to Mark 4:20, the proportion of that harvest depends entirely on you. You can get a thirty, sixty or hundredfold return on the Word sown in your heart. Verse 24 tells us how you can accrue maximum harvest.

"And He said to them, Be careful what you are hearing. The measure [of thought and study] you give [to the truth you

hear] will be the measure [of virtue and knowledge] that comes back to you—and more [besides] will be given to you who hear" (Mark 4:24, Amplified).

This says it all, the measure of meditation and study you give to the Word, will determine the harvest that comes back to you. You must develop a voracious appetite for the Word of God. It carries amazing profit.

Joshua 1:8 reveals the power of meditating on the Word. One man of God says that we should meditate on the Word until we squeeze out all of its juices. Meditating on the Word means to muse, speak, ponder, or declare the Word. Meditation of the Word transforms what you believe. Through meditation, the Word will begin to speak to you. You meditate on it until what you read or what God says becomes more real to you than any situation can speak otherwise. Remember, Mark 4:28 says first the blade; when you start meditating on the Word, things around you will start confirming the fact that it is growing and very soon manifestation will come (the full corn in the ear).

On purpose, I have developed an insatiable appetite for the Word of God. I keep the Word before all my receptors (ear and eye gate). I am either reading the Word of God on a daily basis or listening to a teaching tape (Anointed Word only). Why? First, I have a revelation of the power of the Word of God as I have been conveying to you, and secondly, I have read "The Art of War" by Sun Tzu, whose expert advice is "to know your enemy which will allow you to outsmart and defeat him." The scripture says the devil (my enemy) departs for a season (Luke 4:13); and that he is like a roaring lion seeking whom he may devour (1 Peter 5:8). I cannot afford to allow my spirit to become empty because I realize that it would be just a matter of time before depression and its cousins would return.

Joy Fills the Spirit

The article written for *The Christian Counselor* also revealed that *"Even the most devoted Christian can find themselves slipping into a pattern of not reading the bible as much, not devoting time to worship and praise as much as before. What happens when we don't? A lot. Much can go wrong in our lives, slowly and steadily, we see changes. They are subtle. Evil is subtle. Evil takes advantage of stress, physical pain and emotional sufferings. It takes advantage of our weak points. It loves when we slip, backslide for just a moment. Why? Because that allows it to sneak in, quietly. It comes in the back door so it won't be noticed."*

This is why we must be sober and vigilant (1 Peter 5:8). We must keep ourselves in an attitude of praise.

"Then [Ezra] told them, Go your way, eat the fat, drink the sweet drink, and send portions to him for whom nothing is prepared; for this day is holy to our Lord. And be not grieved and depressed, for the joy of the Lord is your strength and stronghold" (Nehemiah 8:10).

Most of us are familiar with this treasured scripture, "the joy of the Lord is my strength," but why was it written? Nehemiah was adamant about rebuilding the walls of Jerusalem—He was doing a work for the Lord (Nehemiah 1-2). The adversary was attempting to thwart the plan of God (Nehemiah 6:1-2). Satan's attacks were relentless. However, Nehemiah defeated the adversary through his steadfastness, resilience and focus (Nehemiah 6:3), and equally important, he kept praise on his lips. He was not distracted by the noise of the enemy (Psalms 55:3). Notice the Amplified Version says the joy of the Lord is not only our strength but a stronghold (a fortress).

Perhaps you are in your present condition because you have lost your joy. Perhaps, you have become consumed with the cares of this world and it is choking the life out of you. The answer is not to bury your head in the sand; to withdraw, but come out praising God. Your life depends on it. The scripture is clear, God cannot abide in a joyless environment (Psalms 22:3), but Satan can.

Joy: A Safe and Effective Medication

> *"Anxiety in a man's heart weighs it down, but an encouraging word makes it glad" (Proverbs 12:25, Amplified).*
>
> *"A glad heart makes a cheerful countenance, but by sorrow of heart the spirit is broken" (Proverbs 15:13, Amplified).*
>
> *"A happy heart is good medicine and a cheerful mind works healing, but a broken spirit dries up the bones" (Proverbs 17:22, Amplified).*

As a believer, you must always keep your cup running over. You are never to allow your spirit to get empty. This has become an invaluable weapon for me. As a preacher and teacher of the Gospel, I always minister out of the overflow. I never tap into my reserves. Let's solidify this point with this last scripture; it speaks volumes:

> *"Never lag in zeal and in earnest endeavor; be aglow and burning with the Spirit, serving the Lord" (Romans 12:11, Amplified).*

What About Me?   6

CARS

*D*uring the previous chapter, we discussed extensively one of the major causes of depression for the believer and that is not giving enough attention to the Word of God. The second cause is equally as important; too much attention to yourself.

Preoccupation With Oneself

You are probably familiar with Joyce Meyers' rendition of a robot walking around crying, "what about me, what about me, what about me?" She was describing how most Christians behave when they are controlled by their soul. This is a dangerous practice. It is never [never] safe to have a pity party. I can assure you, you will entertain many uninvited guests when you do this; guests that come to crash the party.

What is meant by a preoccupation with oneself? Clearly, if you entertain thoughts such as: no one cares about me; why does everyone except me seem to be blessed; when is my Boaz coming; where's my new house or car; why aren't my children excelling, and the list goes on, then you are unequivocally preoccupied with yourself and depression, if not present, is on the horizon.

Let's discover the heart of the Father concerning this:

*"And He said to all, If any person wills to come after Me,
let him deny himself [disown himself, forget, lose sight of
himself and his own interests, refuse and give up himself]
and take up his cross daily and follow Me [cleave steadfastly
to Me, conform wholly to My example in living and, if need
be, in dying also]. For whoever would preserve his life and
save it will lose and destroy it, but whoever loses his life for
My sake, he will preserve and save it [from the penalty of
eternal death]" (Luke 9:23-24, Amplified).*

As believers this message is not new, but perhaps misunderstood
and therefore neglected. We often hear that we must die so God can
be glorified. But what does it mean to really die? Does it mean that
we no longer have desires; that we don't have feelings or cares; or
that we simply have to "wait on God?" God forbid. As long as we
are in the world, there will be opportunities for growth and develop-
ment through the pressures imposed by the enemy and the world.
What we die to is attempting to take care of ourselves, to analyze
our lives and come up with our own solutions; to try to figure out
everything. God wants you to develop an absolute trust in His love
for you. He wants you to humble yourself under His mighty hand.
Let's explore the true meaning of humility.

*"Therefore humble yourselves [demote, lower yourselves in
your own estimation] under the mighty hand of God, that in
due time He may exalt you, Casting the whole of your care
[all your anxieties, all your worries, all your concerns, once
and for all] on Him, for He cares for you affectionately and
cares about you watchfully" (1 Peter 5:6-7, Amplified).*

The Apostle offers a startling revelation of humility: we are
humble when we give all our cares, anxieties, worries, and concerns
to God. In other words, we are not looking at how we can take care
of things, but rather rely on the God of our salvation. Notice he said

"once and for all," that means we do not take them back once we have released them. God wants us to trust Him.

A humble man (species, not gender) is one who is lowly. When you are lowly, you are submitted to another; submissive. Humility means to reduce your power, your plan, your program, and your independence. Very simply put, it is obedience to the one you are under control (not over). Humility is the picture of a man, lowly man, who recognizes his authority—God—and He goes to God refusing to move until he receives instructions from God on how to move, where to move, when to move, and what to do when he gets there. A humble man will obey the instructions of God. He is strictly dependent upon God's will, God's way, God's programs, God's plans, and God's pursuits.

> *"Whoever will humble himself therefore and become like this little child [trusting, lowly, loving, forgiving] is greatest in the kingdom of heaven" (Matthew 18:4, Amplified).*
> *"Commit your way to the Lord [roll and repose each care of your load on Him]; trust (lean on, rely on, and be confident) also in Him and He will bring it to pass" (Psalms 37:5, Amplified).*
> *"Cast your burden on the Lord [releasing the weight of it] and He will sustain you; He will never allow the [consistently] righteous to be moved (made to slip, fall, or fail)" (Psalms 55:22, Amplified).*

A prideful man, on the other hand, is the reciprocal to the humble man. He has his own program, his own agenda, his own way of getting there, his own time of getting there and does what he wants when he gets there. He refuses to obey or submit to the one in authority—God. He is a man that is in the position of determining his own destiny by his own means and his own ways.

The Plight of the Prideful Man

"For God sets Himself against the proud (the insolent, the overbearing, the disdainful, the presumptuous, the boastful)—[and He opposes, frustrates, and defeats them], but gives grace (favor, blessing) to the humble" (1 Peter 5:5, Amplified).

God cannot do anything with and for you until you relieve yourself of the responsibility of taking care of matters yourself. This world and its declining system are too big for you. Outside the mind and discipline of God, you are no match for the devil. And God says here, He [Himself] resists (opposes, frustrates, and defeats) the proud. But notice God's reaction to the humble:

"But He gives us more and more grace (power of the Holy Spirit, to meet this evil tendency and all others fully). That is why He says, God sets Himself against the proud and haughty, but gives grace [continually] to the lowly (those who are humble enough to receive it)" (James 4:6, Amplified).

"Though He scoffs at the scoffers and scorns the scorners, yet He gives His undeserved favor to the low [in rank], the humble, and the afflicted" (Proverbs 3:34).

The Bible provides a consummate example of the necessity and benefit of not having an exaggerated opinion of ourselves demonstrated by attempting to guide and manage our lives. This dialog will help us understand the extent to which we are to *lay our burdens down.* Jesus is the consummate example of one who, although equal with God, refused to take on the responsibility of self-care.

"I am able to do nothing from Myself [independently, of My own accord—but only as I am taught by God and as I get His orders]. Even as I hear, I judge [I decide as I am bidden

*to decide. As the voice comes to Me, so I give a decision],
and My judgment is right (just, righteous), because I do not
seek or consult My own will [I have no desire to do what
is pleasing to Myself, My own aim, My own purpose] but
only the will and pleasure of the Father Who sent Me"(John
5:30, Amplified).*

*"So Jesus answered them by saying, I assure you, most
solemnly I tell you, the Son is able to do nothing of Himself (of
His own accord); but He is able to do only what He sees the
Father doing, for whatever the Father does is what the Son
does in the same way [in His turn]"(John 5:19, Amplified).*

Jesus Our Example

*"Let this same attitude and purpose and [humble] mind be
in you which was in Christ Jesus: [Let Him be your example
in humility:] Who, although being essentially one with God
and in the form of God [possessing the fullness of the attributes which make God God], did not think this equality with
God was a thing to be eagerly grasped or retained, But
stripped Himself [of all privileges and rightful dignity], so
as to assume the guise of a servant (slave), in that He became
like men and was born a human being. And after He had
appeared in human form, He abased and humbled Himself
[still further] and carried His obedience to the extreme of
death, even the death of the cross! Therefore [because He
stooped so low] God has highly exalted Him and has freely
bestowed on Him the name that is above every name..."
(Philippians 2:5-9, Amplified).*

Oh, what humility. Our Lord and Savior provides a clear
example on how we are to live and conduct our lives while on this
earth. Although essentially one with God, He depended on the
Father for his every move. We know He operated in the gifts of
the Spirit, because He knew man's heart before they uttered words,
yet he made no decisions of his own (Matthew 9:4; John 2: 24-25;

13:11; 16:19). The Apostle Paul admonishes us to *"Let this same attitude and purpose and [humble] mind be in you which was in Christ Jesus: [Let Him be your example in humility:]" (Philippians 2:5, Amplified)."*

Lessons Learned from the Children of Israel

We question the faithlessness of the children of Israel, yet share the same evil report. We commit adultery everyday when we go to the world or pull out our own reserve resources to take care of us (James 4:8). Our Father is quite serious about this:

"WOE TO the rebellious children, says the Lord, who take counsel and carry out a plan, but not Mine, and who make a league and pour out a drink offering, but not of My Spirit, thus adding sin to sin; Who set out to go down into Egypt, and have not asked Me—to flee to the stronghold of Pharaoh and to strengthen themselves in his strength and to trust in the shadow of Egypt! Therefore shall the strength and protection of Pharaoh turn to your shame, and the refuge in the shadow of Egypt be to your humiliation and confusion. For though [Pharaoh's] officials are at Zoan and his ambassadors arrive at Hanes [in Egypt], Yet will all be ashamed because of a people [the Egyptians] who cannot profit them, who are not a help or benefit, but a shame and disgrace. A mournful, inspired prediction (a burden to be lifted up) concerning the beasts of the South (the Negeb): Oh, the heavy burden, the load of treasures going to Egypt! Through a land of trouble and anguish, in which are lioness and lion, viper and fiery flying serpent, they carry their riches upon the shoulders of young donkeys, and their treasures upon the humps of camels, to a people that will not and cannot profit them. For Egypt's help is worthless and toward no purpose. Therefore I have called her Rahab Who Sits Still" (Isaiah 30:1-7, Amplified).

As you recall, for the believer, Egypt is a *type and shadow* of the world and Pharaoh is a *type and shadow* of Satan—the adversary.

But notice Isaiah 30:18, "*And therefore the Lord [earnestly] waits [expecting, looking, and longing] to be gracious to you; and therefore He lifts Himself up, that He may have mercy on you and show loving-kindness to you. For the Lord is a God of justice. Blessed (happy, fortunate, to be envied) are all those who [earnestly] wait for Him, who expect and look and long for Him [for His victory, His favor, His love, His peace, His joy, and His matchless, unbroken companionship]!*" *(Amplified)*.

Why is it so hard for us to trust God? I'll tell you why. It is because we do not have a redemptive revelation of the love of God. It is imperative that we meditate on the scriptures until we get a revelation of the love of God. Until that love is perfected we will walk in fear and fear attracts the devil just as faith attracts God.

> "*There is no fear in love [dread does not exist], but full-grown (complete, perfect) love turns fear out of doors and expels every trace of terror! For fear brings with it the thought of punishment, and [so] he who is afraid has not reached the full maturity of love [is not yet grown into love's complete perfection]. We love Him, because He first loved us*" *(1 John 4:18-19, Amplified)*.

Because the Lord Hated Us?

> "*You were peevish and discontented in your tents, and said, Because the Lord hated us, He brought us forth out of the land of Egypt to deliver us into the hand of the Amorites to destroy us*" *(Deuteronomy 1:27, Amplified)*.

Did the children of Israel actually believe that God hated them? Is not this the same when we question "what about me?" Aren't we saying God loves someone else more, or He doesn't love me enough to do this or that? Take some time to meditate on this. What signal are you sending to the Father because you refuse to trust Him; when you spend many sleepless nights wondering how you will pay your bills, get healed, get married, etc. What are you anxious about?

"Therefore I tell you, stop being perpetually uneasy (anxious and worried) about your life, what you shall eat or what you shall drink; or about your body, what you shall put on. Is not life greater [in quality] than food, and the body [far above and more excellent] than clothing? Look at the birds of the air; they neither sow nor reap nor gather into barns, and yet your heavenly Father keeps feeding them. Are you not worth much more than they? And who of you by worrying and being anxious can add one unit of measure (cubit) to his stature or to the span of his life? And why should you be anxious about clothes? Consider the lilies of the field and learn thoroughly how they grow; they neither toil nor spin. Yet I tell you, even Solomon in all his magnificence (excellence, dignity, and grace) was not arrayed like one of these. But if God so clothes the grass of the field, which today is alive and green and tomorrow is tossed into the furnace, will He not much more surely clothe you, O you of little faith? Therefore do not worry and be anxious, saying, What are we going to have to eat? or, What are we going to have to drink? or, What are we going to have to wear? For the Gentiles (heathen) wish for and crave and diligently seek all these things, and your heavenly Father knows well that you need them all. But seek ye first the kingdom of God, and his righteousness; and all these things shall be added unto you. Take therefore no thought for the morrow: for the morrow shall take thought for the things of itself. Sufficient unto the day is the evil thereof" (Matthew 6:25-34).

God says, "I got this." Then He tells us how in verses 33 and 34:

> *"But seek (aim at and strive after) first of all His kingdom and His righteousness (His way of doing and being right), and then all these things taken together will be given you besides. So do not worry or be anxious about tomorrow, for tomorrow will have worries and anxieties of its own. Sufficient for each day is its own trouble" (Amplified).*

As a believer, you must commit to establishing a healthy, passionate relationship with God so you can develop your trust in Him. You cannot trust someone you do not know (even God). This is the problem with many believers; they simply know God as the Almighty God or "the man upstairs," but not many know Him as a loving Father who longs to take care of you.

Come As Children

> *"I assure you, most solemnly I tell you, when you were young you girded yourself [put on your own belt or girdle] and you walked about wherever you pleased to go. But when you grow old you will stretch out your hands, and someone else will put a girdle around you and carry you where you do not wish to go" (John 21:18, Amplified).*

Listen to the heart of God as we provide a revelation of this scripture. "When you were immature, you said "I can do it myself," but when you became a woman or man, you realized you needed him. You stretched out your hands and allowed God to clothe you and dress you and take you wherever you needed to go.

A Word to the Men:

Brothers, you become a man free from depression and stress when you realize that without God you can do nothing. You must rely on Him, not on the arm of the flesh to take care of your family.

"But I want you to know and realize that Christ is the Head of every man, the head of a woman is her husband, and the Head of Christ is God" (1 Corinthians 11:3).

Yes, you are the man of that house, and God has equipped you (spiritually and physically) to govern your house. But Christ must be your head. In other words, you must rely totally on the power and anointing of God to be that head. You have no wisdom outside the Word of God, John 5:30 must be your resolve. "Honey, I can't do anything but only as I hear from God..." That means you must be a praying man. You must cover your family, especially your children before they walk out of the door. Pray for wisdom on all matters including finances, etc., oftentimes having to say no to your mate who falls prey to emotional spending. But you cannot do this if you are not connected to God (have a strong relationship with Him).

Furthermore, you cannot be connected to God and be enslaved to your place of deployment (your job is really where you have been deployed to change lives and take the wealth of the sinner and bring it to the Kingdom of God). You make your living by sowing (Gen 8:22; Luke 6:38; 2 Cor. 9:6-11). Your job is not your source; God is. You pray for your family, minister the Word to the family, set the standard of living (by the Word) for your family, but this can only be done through the power of God, not your own strength.

"EXCEPT THE Lord builds the house, they labor in vain who build it..." (Psalms 127:1, Amplified).

Although you are the foundation on which your family will stand (picture yourself holding up your family with both your hands), your only sure foundation (that on which you stand), is the Word of God (Matthew 7:24-27). Man of God, the oil flows downward from God the Father, to you, to your family. From there He has commanded the blessing—the empowerment to prosper (Psalms 133:1-2).

I often preach that it was my husband's relationship with God that saved me. It enabled him to know when I needed a husband, a brother, a father, and a lover. This takes the wisdom of God. Had he not culti-vated this, I undoubtedly would not be alive today; I certainly would not be writing this book. Statistics reveal that as many men suffer from depression as women, because they face the same challenges. Of course, we know this is true because the enemy is no respecter of persons. Instead of trying to take on the cares yourself, try this option; grow your faith so you can develop unprecedented trust in the Almighty God. It is only then that you can escape not only depres-sion, but *"the moral decay (rottenness and corruption) that is in the world..." (2 Peter 1:4, Amplified).*

Grow Your Faith

My friend, instead of worrying, take the time to grow your faith. Hebrews 11:6 says that without faith it is impossible to please God. What we lack in the Body of Christ is faith. Do you know that all things considered, all humans are born with the same amount (measure) of muscles. But it is obvious that all of our muscles don't resemble Arnold Swarchenegger or Billy Blanks'. This is because these men spent countless hours developing their muscles. Likewise, we were all dealt the same measure of faith (Romans 12:3). Dr. Frederick K.C. Price, Brother Kenneth Copeland, Sister Joyce Meyer, Dr. Creflo A.

Dollar Jr., and Dr. Bill Winston were not dealt more faith than you and I; that would make God a respecter of persons (Acts 10:34). These individuals are living the abundant life because they have **grown** their faith to that proportion.

How do you grow your faith? Romans 10:17 provides a clear response to this question, *"So then faith cometh by hearing and hearing by the Word of God."* Faith comes by hearing the Word—and **the Word** only. But not just any word—it must be the word of faith (Romans 10:8). If you do not hear faith, you cannot receive faith. For example, if your man or woman of God (Pastor) does not believe in divine healing, they will not teach divine healing. That means you will never develop enough faith to be healed of a sickness. You will continue to depend on medicine or the physicians in your town to heal you. Likewise, if you hear that God doesn't heal everyone or that everyone has to get sick some times, this is what you will develop your faith to receive. What happens when the physicians send you home because they have no cure? You are in deep trouble. This one example alone should stir your spirit to be in a church where the Word of faith is being preached; not where the singing is good, or the carpet is pretty or that's where Big Mama attended church. A clear example of the necessity of hearing the word of faith is demonstrated in Numbers 13 with the twelve preachers that went on a reconnaissance mission.

In Numbers 13:3, Moses sent the leaders (pastors) to scout out the land. They were supposed to return having a faith rally. Instead they brought back an evil report (verse 32) and note the people's reaction:

"All the Israelites grumbled and deplored their situation, accusing Moses and Aaron, to whom the whole congregation said, Would that we had died in Egypt! Or that we had died in this wilderness! Why does the Lord bring us to this land to fall

by the sword? Our wives and little ones will be a prey. Is it not better for us to return to Egypt?"(Numbers 14:2-3)

They did not preach the word of faith, but doubt and unbelief, and the congregation responded in kind. You will never be able to ultimately entrust your life into God's hands without an undeniable trust in Him and you will never muster enough trust in Him without faith. Every care, every concern you have; your marriage, sexual bliss, business ventures, loneliness, finances, guilt, shame, distresses, etc., they are no match for God. He is after all, El Shaddai, the all-sufficient God and El Elyon, the Most High God. You can't "grow wings like a dove and fly away and be at rest." You have to trust God and believe His Word.

The Bible is quite clear how we are to conduct our lives as Christians. When we step outside of the Word of God and rely on our own wisdom, we leave the umbrella of protection that is provided by the blood of Jesus. Again, God is your Father and he wants the sole responsibility of taking care of you. God led the Children of Israel out in the wilderness where there was nothing, to teach them to depend on Him for everything, including their bare essentials.

One of the most gratifying fringe benefits we have as believers is we get to retire from works. Meditate on these scriptures until they begin to speak to you louder than the cares of this world; until what you have in your heart becomes more real than the situations you are facing, then throw yourself a retirement party. I guarantee that you won't have any uninvited or unexpected guests this time. They'll be tied up at their command post explaining to the devil how they allowed you to get out of their grip. We're almost there; let's peel off the layers of our stinking thinking and uncontrolled emotions.

The Unrestrained Thought Life   *7*

*N*o book on depression would be complete without a discussion on the correlation between one's thoughts and depression. We must examine ourselves, and look at what consumes our thoughts and what we are releasing out of our mouths. Your thought life plays an integral role in the success and failures in your life.

Let's examine a scripture that was instrumental in setting me free from depression:

> *"All the days of the desponding and afflicted are made evil [by anxious thoughts and forebodings], but he who has a glad heart has a continual feast [regardless of circumstances]"(Proverbs 15:15, Amplified).*

This scripture exposes how the spirit of depression finds an entry point. Notice your days are not evil, but **made** evil. That means it's a process; that there are stages of depression. It starts out with a thought, but as you dwell (meditate) on these thoughts they become thoughts of anxiety. Forebodings are bad feelings, or apprehensions; a fear of what may happen. You may not realize it, but you are setting in motion a spiritual law, "what you fear the most will come upon on you." It is a form of negative meditation. The Old Testament provides an excellent example of this in the book of Job.

"And it was so, when the days of their feasting were gone about, that Job sent and sanctified them, and rose up early in the morning, and offered burnt offerings according to the number of them all: for Job said, It may be that my sons have sinned, and cursed God in their hearts. Thus did Job continually" (Job 1:5).

Job had gotten into a religious place where he prayed (out of fear) for his children not to sin against God and began to perform sacrifices for them. This was Job's greatest fear, one that he meditated on day and night. What was the result?

"While he was yet speaking, there came also another, and said, Thy sons and thy daughters were eating and drinking wine in their eldest brother's house: And, behold, there came a great wind from the wilderness, and smote the four corners of the house, and it fell upon the young men, and they are dead; and I only am escaped alone to tell thee" (Job 1:18-19).

Why did this happen?

"For the thing which I greatly feared is come upon me, and that which I was afraid of is come unto me. I was not in safety, neither had I rest, neither was I quiet; yet trouble came" (Job 3:25-26).

So, it was Job that caused his children's death, not God. We must consider this scripture very carefully, for it reveals how we can partake in the demise of our loved ones. Let's say you fear that when your mate goes to the mall they are going to get hurt; you meditate on this every time they are gone "too" long. You continue to meditate on this until fear is birthed, and then you begin to speak it. You are setting up your mate for potential injury.

The sad thing is, where do you think Job got that thought? It came from the pit of hell. Satan fed him that thought and he bought it. So, it matters what you allow to linger in your mind. Brother Kenneth Hagin would often say, "You can't stop the birds from flying over your head, but you can certainly stop them from building a nest in your hair." You must understand that it is not a small thing to allow a single "ungodly" thought to linger in your mind, for it will become lasciviousness.

"And when he was entered into the house from the people, his disciples asked him concerning the parable. And he saith unto them, Are ye so without understanding also? Do ye not perceive, that whatsoever thing from without entereth into the man, it cannot defile him; Because it entereth not into his heart, but into the belly, and goeth out into the draught, purging all meats? And he said, That which cometh out of the man, that defileth the man. For from within, out of the heart of men, proceed evil thoughts, adulteries, fornications, murders, Thefts, covetousness, wickedness, deceit, lasciviousness, an evil eye, blasphemy, pride, foolishness: All these evil things come from within, and defile the man" (Mark 7:17-23).

What does this parable mean? It says that it is not what comes into a man that defiles him, for example, it is not the food you eat that can corrupt you because it enters into your belly not your heart. Rather, it is that which comes out of a man's heart that defiles a man. Matthew 15:19 says it emphatically, *"For out of the heart proceed evil thoughts, murders, adulteries, fornications, thefts, false witness, blasphemies."* These things come from within.

The enemy knows this and he plays the game very well. He knows he has no power over you so he tries to get you to use your own authority against yourself through deception.

Lasciviousness, in Mark 4:22, has to do with having no restraint — something that is unrestrained. What Satan does is try to get you to have no restraint on your thinking. He tries to plant a thought in your mind that will give birth to words. He deceives people in thinking things like a thought is so small or it carries no weight. So, he'll shoot a thought in your mind and you'll not think anything about it. However, for that thought to run unrestrained through your mind is dangerous. He will help keep it there. He'll even use relatives or friends, anyone, to help keep thoughts there. You must understand that his main goal is to affect the will of God for your life. This is what happens when you allow your thoughts to go unchecked.

"Follow peace with all men, and holiness, without which no man shall see the Lord: Looking diligently lest any man fail of the grace of God; lest any root of bitterness springing up trouble you, and thereby many be defiled" (Hebrews 12:14-15).

Let's use offense to expose how Satan uses unrestrained thoughts to trap you. Let's say someone has offended you in some way. It starts with a small thought. You begin to think, "Why did this person do that to me?" Satan tries to get you to think about it. When you think about it, you develop it and when you develop it, it begins to sink down into your soul; it begins to grow up on the inside. When it begins to grow up on the inside, the thought begins to start controlling your speech and you begin to start saying things that are relative to this thought. If you had let it go, taking it and casting down that imagination because it exalted itself against the

Word of God (2 Corinthians 10:4-6), then Satan wouldn't be able to control you. You are well aware that the Word says you should forgive this person but you have thought about it so long, and when it first entered your mind, Satan said it was just a little thought, then the next thing, bitterness sprung up and the thoughts begin to control you and you begin to justify why you are mad. You begin to say, they should have never done this. Now he has you where he wants you because it is hard to get out of this unharmed because there is a root of bitterness in there.

If you are thinking obsessively about something, running it over in your mind that is called lasciviousness; you have no restraints to your thinking. This is how depression starts. You begin to feel sorry for yourself.

"Anxiety in a man's heart weighs it down, but an encouraging word makes it glad"(Proverbs 12:25-26).

You must get the devil off your trail. The devil has been messing with your mind and you thought it was just a little thought and you kept thinking about it and have created a giant—lasciviousness. You have allowed that thought to run in your mind unrestrained allowing it to take root in you, thus controlling your speech and very life. It's all you can think about. That's how adultery takes place, homosexuality, etc. You never captured the thought the enemy fed you.

How does this apply to depression? Let's say you are concerned about your health, business, marriage, children, employment, relationships, etc., and the devil planted a thought in your mind of your demise. If you've spent time meditating on this, it has now become a stronghold, a root. These thoughts start manifesting in your dreams, in your speech, in your actions. Because you feel hopeless (have created an environment of hopelessness through your thoughts), what follows is depression that has you on a downward spiral and you don't know how you got there. Your actions will fall in line with your words and your words will fall in line with your thoughts, if you continue to entertain those thoughts and repeat them in your mind.

Let me share with you one of the greatest scriptures that revolutionized my life about my thoughts:

"The thoughts of the righteous are right: but the counsels of the wicked are deceit" (Proverbs 12:5).

You are the righteousness of God (Romans 5:17-19; 2 Corinthians 5:21), so this scripture means that any thought that comes to your mind that does not line up with the Word of God is not your thought. Have you ever had a thought come to your mind that caused you to question your salvation? In other words, you asked yourself what could be wrong with me thinking such despicable thoughts. The answer is simple, they're not your thoughts.

Several years ago, when I lived in the Philippines, I repeatedly heard a voice telling me to run my car into a tree. I really thought I was losing my mind, until one day a visiting preacher ministered a message about the "uncrucified thought life." He mentioned how oftentimes, for no apparent reason, he would get this thought to run his car into a tree or off a cliff. He mentioned how Satan attempts to plant a seed in your mind and is counting on you to give birth to it by meditating on it then releasing it out of your mouth. He shared the revelation of Proverbs 12:5. Of course, I was flabbergasted. I knew then that this was not my thought but Satan's thought and this revelation has saved my life. Just recently someone told me of this pastor's wife, who is suffering from depression, hearing a voice telling her to run her car into a tree. I shook my head saying he's still using the same tactics. We are no longer ignorant of the devil's devices (2 Corinthians 2:11). We now know what to do with these thoughts.

> *"But test and prove all things [until you can recognize] what is good; [to that] hold fast" (1 Thessalonians 5:21, Amplified).*
>
> *"For the rest, brethren, whatever is true, whatever is worthy of reverence and is honorable and seemly, whatever is just, whatever is pure, whatever is lovely and lovable, whatever is kind and winsome and gracious, if there is any virtue and excellence, if there is anything worthy of praise, think on and weigh and take account of these things [fix your minds on them]." (Philippians 4:8, Amplified).*
>
> *"For the weapons of our warfare are not physical [weapons of flesh and blood], but they are mighty before God for the overthrow and destruction of strongholds, [Inasmuch as we] refute arguments and theories and reasonings and every proud and lofty thing that sets itself up against the [true] knowledge of God; and we lead every thought and purpose away captive into the obedience of Christ (the Messiah, the Anointed one" (2 Corinthians 10:4-5, Amplified).*
>
> *"The thoughts of the diligent tend only to plenteousness; but of every one that is hasty only to want" (Proverbs 21:5).*

Your thoughts should edify you. The Hebrew word for plenteousness is *mowthar*, which means to gain; superiority; preeminence; profit; to exceed; to excel; cause to abound; too much. So you should receive and meditate only on those thoughts that edify you or others. Any other thoughts should be dismissed because they are not your thoughts.

And we must be adamant about what we allow to enter our ear and eye gates. I cannot say enough about this. Proverbs 4:23 says,

"Keep and guard your heart with all vigilance and above all that you guard , for out of it flow the springs of life."

Recently, I was watching a documentary on the effects of Crystal Methamphetamine abuse in a small Montana town. The effects were distressing. I could feel the weight of the world attempting to perch itself on my compassionate shoulders. Through teary eyes, I immediately recognized the plaguing thoughts, prayed for all of those gripped by drugs and confessed the Word of prosperity over me so my husband and I could build facilities to assist people in getting free from substance abuse (one of the goals of our Community Resource Center). I recognized the devil's tactics and withstood him at his onset.

We are not built to carry cares. We cannot save [all] the whales, the world from global warming, or the like. Something as subtle as this invites depression; we must guard our hearts with all diligence. My resolve has become, "if it (whatever the situation is) doesn't benefit the kingdom of God, I have no room for it."

The Power of the Tongue

Another powerful revelation that will help you immensely, is understanding how Satan tries to get your thoughts to give birth to your words.

"If you have done foolishly in exalting yourself, or if you have thought evil, lay your hand upon your mouth" (Proverbs 10:32).

The author is warning you that if you have thought an evil thought (any thought that does not line up with the Word of God, i.e., how am I going to buy school clothes for the kids, how can I survive cancer when everyone knows there is no cure, why doesn't my husband love me, etc—), the first thing you should do is lay your hand over your mouth, i.e., not allow these thoughts to escape your lips. Why, because ultimately the enemy knows that he wants to play out your thoughts through your life and he knows that your words are key to doing that. Remember he knows scripture also. He knows that life and death are in the power of your tongue (Proverbs 18:21). What he wants you to do is operate in unrestrained thoughts.

No one is exempt from the devil's ruthless tactics. He is not concerned with your genuineness or honesty, in fact he hates you because you not only love God, but you represent what he once had—unending fellowship with God. He will use whatever is in his bag of tricks with your name on it to destroy you (John 10:10). Jesus called the devil an evil genius (John 14:30, Amplified) and he is certainly no respecter of persons. He will lay a trap by shooting a thought in your head and if you do not immediately cast down that thought, you are open prey for him. Let me give you an example.

Maybe I Should Marry Charlie

Again, while I was living in the Philippines several years ago, I had become somewhat overburdened with my military and Christian responsibilities. Not only was I the Wing Intelligence Officer at a fighter wing that carried enormous responsibilities; the Pastor of a church in Negrito Village, Philippines, and the Assistant Pastor at my home church in the same area; but also a single parent. One night as I was locking up after a long day at the base, I began to think how lonely I was, how "everybody had someone but me, why was I alone, didn't anyone want me?" I remember distinctly opening my mouth and saying, "maybe I should marry Charlie, he's not so bad, after all he's my daughter's father." You are probably gasping as you should be. Of course, I didn't know what I know now and what I am sharing with you about Proverbs 10:32. That was certainly an evil thought. My ex-husband at that time was a recovering heroin addict of over 20 years. These words put Satan's plan into motion.

It was Satan who shot those thoughts in my mind. My response should have been one of encouragement, "My times are in thy hand..." (Psalms 31:15) or "there is a time for everything...." (Ecclesiastes 3:1-8) and that would have been the end of it. Instead, I watched the couples in church and at the restaurants, and I pondered when Lord, when, after all I was in my thirties and never married. I watered my pillow with my tears. I allowed those thoughts to give birth to words and the downward spiral in my life began immediately, almost resulting in my death.

The words that we speak can produce life or death; they can be positive or negative; they can encourage or discourage.

> "You are snared with the Words of your lips, you are caught by the speech of your mouth" (Proverbs 6:2, Amplified).
> "Death and life are in the power of the tongue: and they that love it shall eat the fruit thereof" (Proverbs 18:21).
> "A man's belly shall be satisfied with the fruit of his mouth; and with the increase of his lips shall he be filled" (Proverbs 18:20).

That means I can control my own destiny, simply by deliberately watching what comes out of my mouth. I can destroy or edify my life by my words—it is as simple as that. Are we back to that; watching our words, you ask? When did we depart from this revelation?

James 3:3-5 says, *"If we set bits in the horses' mouths to make them obey us, we can turn their whole bodies about. Likewise, look at the ships: though they are so great and are driven by rough winds, they are steered by a very small rudder wherever the impulse of the helmsman determines. Even so the tongue is a little member, and it can boast of great things. See how much wood or how great a forest a tiny spark can set ablaze!"*

The Apostle James teaches us that the tongue is like a rudder on a ship, or a bit in a horse's mouth. By turning a rudder you can guide a huge vessel. Or, by pulling the reins attached to the bit in a horse's mouth, you can control his direction. What is the lesson here? Your tongue is a powerful instrument; it can chart the course of your life; it can produce life or death. You must watch what you say under pressure. The Word of God is emphatic about the power of the believer's words.

James 3:6-11 says, *"And the tongue is a fire, a world of iniquity: so is the tongue among our members, that it defileth the whole body, and setteth on fire the course of nature; and is set on fire of hell, for every kind of beast, and of birds, and of serpents, and of things in the sea, is tamed, and hath been tamed of mankind: But the tongue can no man tame; it is an unruly evil, full of deadly poison. Therewith bless we God, even the Father; and therewith curse we men, which are made after the similitude of God. Out of the same mouth proceedeth blessing and cursing. My brethren, these things ought not so to be. Doth a fountain send forth at the same place sweet water and bitter?" (Amplified).*

The Apostle Paul says in 1 Corinthians 2:4-5:

"And my language and my message were not set forth in persuasive (enticing and plausible) words of wisdom, but they were in demonstration of the [Holy] Spirit and power [a proof by the Spirit and power of God, operating on me and stirring in the minds of my hearers the most holy emotions and thus persuading them], So that your faith might not rest in the wisdom of men (human philosophy), but in the power of God" (Amplified).

Matthew 12:37 is quite clear, it says "for by **your** words you will be justified and acquitted, and by **your** words you will be condemned and sentenced." In other words, you determine your own verdict.

Finally, let's not forget that the Word of God says, *"But I tell you, on the day of judgment men will have to give account for every idle (inoperative, nonworking) word they speak"* (Matthew 12:36, Amplified).

Positive Side of Words

We can see there is a negative, dark side, but there is always a positive, light side as well.

"The mouth of a righteous man is a well of life..." (Proverbs 10:11).

"In the lips of him that hath understanding wisdom is found: but a rod is for the back of him that is void of understanding" (Proverbs 10:13).

"The tongue of the just is as choice silver..." (Proverbs 10:20).

"A wholesome tongue is a tree of life..." (Proverbs 15:4).

"The lips of the righteous feed many..." (Proverbs 10:21).

"A man hath joy by the answer of his mouth: and a word spoken in due season, how good is it!" (Proverbs 15:23).

The Law of Confession

While I'm here let me add a brief discussion about confessing the Word of God. No, I am not speaking of one of the Catholic Sacraments of Reconciliations, but the *law* of confession available to the Body of Christ.

A law is an established principle that works all the time, and will work for whoever will apply that law. The law of gravity, which says, "What goes up must come down," is an example of this. The Word of God also works by established principles, or laws. For example, in the Body of Christ we have the law of faith, the law of sowing and reaping and the law of confession, to name a few. The law of confession works like this:

"Thou shalt also decree a thing, and it shall be established unto thee: and the light shall shine upon thy ways" (Job 22:28).

Decree is used here to pronounce or confess.

There is a connection between what you say and what you have. It is obvious that believers have not made that connection. We know that because we say "my feet are killing me," or when we're hot we say, "I'm burning up." I've been corrected on this several times. We obviously have not made the connection that we can have what we say. Words are not just noise, they are spirit (John 6:63) and the spiritual things govern natural things. Our words that are spirit are meant to govern our natural world. Your words have value. You can actually speak things and the things you speak will manifest.

"And Jesus, replying, said to them, Have faith in God [constantly]. Truly I tell you, whoever says to this mountain, Be lifted up and thrown into the sea! and does not doubt at

*all in his heart but believes that what he says will take place,
it will be done for him. For this reason I am telling you,
whatever you ask for in prayer, believe (trust and be confi-
dent) that it is granted to you, and you will [get it]"(Mark
11:22-24, Amplified).*

Jesus is establishing a spiritual law here. He is saying you can
have whatever you say when you pray (as long as you believe you
can). Well, when you pray you have to open your mouth. Words
must proceed from your mouth. Again, the scripture says, "My
people perish for lack of knowledge" (Hosea 4:6). We practice
things that are totally unscriptural, like silent prayers. What are
silent prayers? This world is governed by words. We must open
our mouths and speak. Try going to McDonalds and staring at the
cashier and believing that through osmosis they know your order.
That's ridiculous. The Bible says we can have what we say.

This is very essential teaching. Positive thinking alone is not
enough. But if you don't apply action or confessions to it, you'll
still sink. In other words, the boat is still going down, you're just
smiling as you sink. We want to get positive thinking coupled with
the words that we speak and the actions we take. Your confessions
are essential.

Releasing faith-filled words can produce manifestation and
bring you the zoe life. This is one of the laws I practiced to get
free. Every time depression would appear at my door I immediately
began to pray in the spirit and immediately started making "Word"
confessions such as, Lord your Word says I can have what I say, so
I declare that:

- *I am the righteousness of God*
- *My life has been redeemed from destruction*

- *I'll never be depressed another day in my life*
- *I'll never be downtrodden another day in my life*
- *I'll never be consumed with cares another day in my life*
- *I'll never be sick another day in my life*
- *The joy of the Lord is my strength*
- *I can do all things through Christ who strengthens me.....*

To this day, I make daily "Word" confessions and my life has changed radically. It doesn't matter how I feel when I am making those confessions; I know that the law of confession is taking affect. The law is working now, even though I may not see change immediately, things are working.

Brother Charles Capps, an acclaimed authority on the "tongue as a creative force," says that "Spoken words program your spirit either to success or defeat." Words are containers, he intimates. They carry faith or fear, and they produce after their kind. The Word of God says, "So faith cometh by hearing and hearing by the Word of God" (Romans 10:17). Brother Capps reveals that faith comes more quickly when you hear yourself quoting, speaking, and saying the things God said. In other words, you will more readily receive God's Word into your spirit by hearing yourself say it than if you hear someone else say it. Why? Your body was created by God to respond to messages received from **your mouth**. That when it hears **you say** something it postures itself to respond.

So confession is treatment within itself. When you confess the Word, you are putting spiritual law into motion. Start your road to total victory by establishing some "Word" confessions to speak over you and your family daily. You can begin by using the scriptures I have presented in this book and your prosperity (spirit, soul, and body) is guaranteed.

I am not advocating that if you are on medication, that you throw away or discard your medicine and rely on confession alone unless the Lord directs you to do so. As I said previously, it takes time to renew your mind and develop faith in your words as well as God's Word. But the things you are continually confessing will eventually become a part of you. You can appropriate healing and restoration in every area of your life by making the Word a part of your daily vocabulary.

For a complete study on this subject, order "The Tongue, A Creative Force; God's Creative Power; and God's Creative Power for Healing," all by Charles Capps. You can access his website at www.charlescapps.com.

Those Darn Emotions   *8*

*J*ust as your thoughts and words (tongue) can direct your life, so can your emotions. Let's review our previous discussion about the tripartite nature of man. According to 1 Thessalonians 5:23, man has a tripartite nature. Man is a spirit, has a soul and lives in a body. Mistakenly, the soul and spirit have been used interchangeably. It is imperative that we understand they are different entities and possess different functions. Genesis 1:26 reveals the creation of man. God said, "Let us make man in our image and after our likeness." Our Lord and Savior tells us that God is a spirit (John 4:24), so since we are made in the image of God, we can safely say we are spirit. That part of us (spirit) is just like God, but it leaves two parts, our soul and body. The body is just the catalyst used to navigate us physically through the earth, submitting to which of the other two are in control. That leaves the soul.

We have discussed in length the danger of not taming your soul and it becomes even clearer here. Let's concentrate on this area of the soul as it pertains to your emotions. Third John 2 says something profound about the soul: *"Beloved, I wish above all things that thou mayest prosper and be in health, even as thy soul prospereth."*

The Apostle is saying as your soul goes, so goes your life. In other words, you mastering life is directionally proportionate to the prosperity of your soul. Your soul, as you recall, consists of your mind, will, and emotions. Your mind is your thinking apparatus. Proverbs 23:7 says, "*As a man thinketh in his heart, so is he.*" Your will is your chooser. God made us all free moral agents with the right to choose the course of our lives. Joshua 24:15 says, "*And if it seems evil to you to serve the Lord, choose for yourselves this day whom you will serve.*" Therefore, we have a will so we can choose. The final area of our soul is our emotions or feelings.

Unfortunately, in Christendom, we have not spent much time talking about our feelings, and the result has been catastrophic. We must learn to master our emotions, because our mastering life begins with our controlling our emotions—our feelings. Yes, God gave us emotions; the problem arises when we allow those emotions to control us. So, does that mean we are not supposed to have emotions? God forbid! We could not love the Father or each other without them. In fact God designed us to have emotions and passions, but they are not supposed to **have** us. We must understand how imperative it is to learn to control our feelings and emotions because if you can control your emotions, you can do exactly anything. Let's validate this point.

Proverbs 16:32 says, "*He that is slow to anger is better than the mighty; and he that ruleth his spirit than he that taketh a city.*"

Now it is important that we do an exegesis of this scripture. Here we see that even bible scholars have made the error of using the spirit and soul interchangeably. The word "spirit" here in the original text is translated *ruwach*, which means mind, the exercise of mental power, the seat of emotion. So, a better translation of this "spirit" is "mind." Well, the mind is part of the soul. So this scripture should actually read: He that is slow to anger is better than the mighty; *and he that rules his soul is better than he that takes a city.* Do you see that? If you can control your emotions you are like an army that can take over a city.

Let's define emotions. In Latin, "E" is translated up, out, and away; "motions" is self explanatory, it denotes movement. We know that emotions are associated with feelings, so a practical explanation of emotions is "feelings on the inside that can move you in a certain direction." Its purpose is to move you in a certain direction. Do you realize that you can have holy emotions or perverted emotions?

First Corinthians 2:4-5 says, *"And my language and my message were not set forth in persuasive (enticing and plausible) words of wisdom, but they were in demonstration of the [Holy] Spirit and power [a proof by the Spirit and power of God, operating on me and stirring in the minds of my hearers the most holy emotions and thus persuading them], So that your faith might not rest in the wisdom of men (human philosophy), but in the power of God"* (Amplified).

When you live by the Word of God, you will have holy emotions that are designed to move you in the direction of the will of God. Likewise, if your thinking is contrary to the Word of God, then you will have emotions that will move you against the will of God. Why is this important? Jesus called Satan an evil genius (John 14:30, Amplified). He may not have access to your body, but he can certainly gain a foothold if he can get you to be controlled by your *untamed* emotions. If he can seduce your emotions, then he can move you out of the will of God. Many of us have taken unfortunate and lengthy detours due to this perversion. Our emotions have gotten many of us in trouble and this is one of the major causes of depression. Let's discuss how Jesus controlled His emotions.

Hebrews 4:15 says, *"For we have not an high priest which cannot be touched with the feeling of our infirmities; but was in all points tempted like as we are, yet without sin."*

This scripture confirms that Jesus also had emotions, but His emotions never had Him, thank God. They never moved Him away from the will of God. Yes, Jesus can relate to your feelings, He has experienced the same feelings — He understands your pains and sorrows; there are no feelings you've had, or currently have, that Jesus hasn't experienced; yet He never allowed those feelings to move Him away from God's will (Isaiah 53:4-5; Philippians 2:7-8; Heb 4:15).

Jesus cultivated the ability to control His feelings and the result was providential. Let's read Mark 14:32-34:

> *"Then they went to a place called Gethsemane, and He said to His disciples, Sit down here while I pray. And He took with Him Peter and James and John, and began to be struck with terror and amazement and deeply troubled and **depressed**. And He said to them, My soul is exceedingly sad (overwhelmed with grief) so that it almost kills Me! Remain here and keep awake and be watching"* (Amplified).

Luke's gospel says, *"And being in an agony [of mind], He prayed [all the] more earnestly and intently, and His sweat became like great clots of blood dropping down upon the ground,"* (*Luke 22:44, Amplified*).

What was going on here? His emotions were under great attack. Remember in the movie, "The Passion of the Christ," Satan and his demons were depicted in the garden spewing fiery darts (suggestions) at Jesus to see if they could move Him away from the will of God. Satan knows scripture; he knows the will of God for your life, probably more than you do, and he is standing by to move you away from the will of God. Although Jesus was severely attacked, He stayed in the will of God (Luke 22:42). Do you see the importance of not allowing your emotions to control you?

Finally, let's deal with this area of hurt and pain. Somehow, we feel justified to stay in bitterness and anger (emotions) if someone has hurt us and this again can cause a permanent detour in your life.

The Apostle Paul says:

"Brethren, I count not myself to have apprehended: but this one thing I do, forgetting those things which are behind, and reaching forth unto those things which are before, I press toward the mark for the prize of the high calling of God in Christ Jesus"(Philippians 3:13).

Again, let's perform an exegesis of this scripture. In the Authorized Version, the words "this" and "I do" are italicized, which mean that these words were added by the translators, a privilege granted to them to bring clarity. However, look at what happens when we remove these words. It would read: "Brethren I count not myself to have apprehended but one thing, forgetting those things which are behind and reaching forth unto those things which are before, I press toward the mark for the prize of the high calling of God in Christ Jesus." Do you see why we must not only read the Word, but allow the Holy Spirit to guide us into the truth of God's Word?

Too many Christians are stuck in their past. If you are holding on to things that happened to you, you are hurt. Hurt people are very angry people and this is a root cause of depression. If you sit around and constantly ponder what someone did to you—how your ex cheated on you, how someone molested or abused you or your children, how someone misused you, how your spouse tries to control you; you are hurt, you are stuck, and depression waits to control your life. Anger is feared based and can cause you to build up a wall that is impenetrable even by God. What past hurt is controlling you? What war scar are you constantly massaging or exposing? Do you realize that if you develop a sore and put a band aid on it, it will never heal? You need to release those individuals and move on with your life; chances are they have moved on with theirs.

My ex-husband became scandalous when the drugs overtook his life. He did unthinkable, horrible things to not only violate our marriage, but endanger our family. And the worse, believe it or not, was not exposing me to the HIV virus. The more I felt sorry for myself, the angrier I became. When I married my current husband, the man of my dreams, he was dealing with an angry and bitter woman, camouflaged with the most refined religious mask ever donned. Only the truth from his lips, the Word of God, delivered me from my past (if you are single, you definitely want a Holy Ghost filled, word of faith believing mate, who will minister truth, not someone who will minister to your emotions). I am now free to love and be loved. What's in your heart?

If you don't close the door to your past, you are an accident waiting to happen. Your emotions will get the best of you and may be exacted toward some motorist who flips you the bird, or some poor cashier who was having a bad day and didn't address you properly or give you the right order, so you went off and lost your witness; or perhaps you find out that your husband is cheating on you and you re-enact a scene from Terry McMillan's book "Waiting To Exhale."

Cast Your Cares Once and for All

This is not the way you master life; this is life mastering you. Come on, let's close the door to your past together. Take all the guilt, hurts, pains, and shame that you have, write them down on a piece of paper, ball them up in your hand, and cast them **once and for all** over on the Lord (you could actually do this by placing them in a garbage pail labeled "Almighty God"). Get you some Word seed, i.e., open your mouth and declare, "According to Psalms 55:22, Lord I release the weight of this burden over on you." Then take the trash out of your sight, take communion over this, and never, ever take back these cares. The trash is already out. Once you've done this, start enjoying your life, your mate, your friends. Knock down those steel walls.

I just heard a nevertheless, so let's briefly deal with the *neverthelesses*. Because Satan is always standing by to resist the believer, he will whisper to you that you need somehow to protect yourself from future hurts and pain even though you have shut the door to your past. Remember, hurt is fear based.

Luke 10:19 is a profound promise for the believer:

"Behold! I have given you authority and power to trample upon serpents and scorpions, and [physical and **mental strength** *and ability] over all the power that the enemy [possesses]; and nothing shall in any way harm you"* (Amplified).

You can be emotionally invincible. When you gave your life to Christ, He promised you that nothing in any way will harm you.

A Note on Toxic Love

Associated with hurts and pains is this area I call toxic love. The scripture says our hope must be in God (Psalms 42:5, 11; 43:5; 78:7). You may have a best friend, husband or child (children) that "mean the world to you." Yes, God designed marriage and He anointed your womb to bring forth offspring from that marriage, but these blessings (gifts) cannot and must not take a place in your heart reserved only for God. This can be to your demise.

If you have developed a love so strong for your mate and your child (children) or anyone, that if they disappoint you so severely, or more catastrophically if they should die prematurely, that you become desperately depressed, nonfunctional, and unfruitful, then you have cultivated toxic love that must be submitted to the will of God. Guard your heart because out of it flows the issues of life (Proverbs 4:23). That means what governs our lives is not what happens outside but inside. If your meditation is "I don't know what I would do if something were to happen to so and so," then lay your hand over your mouth. Capture those thoughts as they, especially once spoken, can release the power of Satan in your life or the life of your loved ones. Remember, out of the abundance of the heart, the mouth speaks (Matthew 12:34). That means if you meditate on something long enough that thought will eventually come out of your mouth. Once this happens, it releases valuable information to the enemy to use against you.

You were created in the image of God to have dominion. He designed you to master life; to reflect His power. Get back into faith and see how good life can be. The layers have been removed, the core exposed, now it's time for you to enjoy life; after all, your life has been redeemed from destruction.

A Life Redeemed From Destruction

9

*A*s we near the completion of this book, it is imperative that we deal with this area of depression so we can position ourselves to complete our assignment on this earth. Everything necessary for us to rule and reign in life has already been completed. So, what's the problem? The problem is ignorance; ignorance of the plan of God for our lives and Satan's strategies for thwarting that plan.

Satan is a defeated foe. Colossians 2:15 says, *"[God] disarmed the principalities and powers that were ranged against us and made a bold display and public example of them, in triumphing over them in Him and in it [the cross]" (Amplified).* He simply preys on those who are ignorant of his devices. He loves to play with your head. This reminds me of a graphic, yet apropos incident I witnessed that convinced me that I *must* live the kingdom life.

While visiting New York several years ago, I remember waking up one morning to noise in the adjoining room. I positioned myself in the bed to investigate what this was. I noticed that in the kitchen, the house cat was playing a swatting match with a mouse (think of

Maria Sharapova's commercial where she is swatting balls from a tennis machine). The mouse was trying desperately to escape but to no avail. The interesting thing is while the cat clearly overpowered the mouse, he didn't devour him, he just kept taunting him. The mouse would try to escape and the cat would take his paw and swat him back where he wanted him. To my disgust this occurred over several minutes until I had had enough and awakened my husband to observe what was going on and "to do something about this fiasco." He ended it quickly by throwing a shoe in the kitchen which startled them both and caused them to scatter.

Initially, I was appalled. This was actually my parent's home and because my parents were elderly, the mice had become squatters, defying them due to their physical limitations. But then it made an indelible imprint on my mind. It made me despise poverty in the fiercest way. It made me hate religion because although I had been in church nearly 20 years, there was no teaching of the necessity of wealth for believers, therefore no faith was released and I couldn't help my parents out of this atrocity. Only the truth, not religion can make you free. This experience accelerated my desire to allow God to complete the work in my life so I could be used to set others free. This is why I am adamant about telling the truth found in the Word of God. My dad has since changed his address to heaven. But by being the solitary in the family (Psalms 68:6) and knowing my kingdom rights, through the power of prayer and God's favor, my mom is now the proprietor of a newly built fabulous home in Covington, Georgia, free from squatters of any kind. My point? Just as that cat was taunting that mouse, Satan taunts the people of God who walk in ignorance. You must evict him now. Remember, he has already been defeated.

As a believer, you must know that through the precious blood of Jesus, your life has been redeemed from destruction.

Galatians 3:13-14 says, *"Christ hath redeemed us from the curse of the law, being made a curse for us: for it is written, Cursed is every one that hangeth on a tree: That the blessing of Abraham might come on the Gentiles through Jesus Christ; that we might receive the promise of the Spirit through faith."* The word *redeemed* is defined as the repurchase of captured goods. That means Christ had to repurchase us from something. Let's find out what that is.

"Wherefore, as by one man sin entered into the world, and death by sin; and so death passed upon all men, for that all have sinned: (For until the law sin was in the world: but sin is not imputed when there is no law. Nevertheless death reigned from Adam to Moses, even over them that had not sinned after the similitude of Adam's transgression, who is the figure of him that was to come" (Romans 5:12-14).

This scripture is rehearsing the first three chapters of the book of Genesis. In Genesis 1, God created a place for man with the best of everything in it (Gen 1:1-25). It was not until He approved what He made for man (ensured it was good enough) that He created man (Adam, the first man) in His image and gave him instructions to take dominion (Gen 1:26). In chapter two, Adam demonstrated that he did in fact have the inner qualities of God; he assisted in creation, confirming that God's plan worked (Gen 2:19-20). God also gave Adam a wife to be a help mate (Gen 2:21-23). Instead, Adam's unholy emotions for her led him away from the will of God and the result was cataclysmic (Gen 3:1-6). Adam's disobedience changed not only the rulership of the earth (he handed it over to Satan), but more profoundly, his sin changed the nature of man; Adam was no longer like God (Gen 3:7-10).

The transfer of rulership to Satan was not the pivotal event in the third chapter of Genesis. It was that man was no longer like God and therefore could not fellowship and partake with Him, the very reason for his existence. The fundamental error we make is God never related to man because of his actions, but based on his nature. God hung out with Adam because Adam was just like God. When he sinned, his nature changed so God could no longer hang with him. However, Romans 5:12-21 is the greatest love story written for men. God's mind never changed about His plan for His creation, man (Numbers 23:19; Hebrews 6:6-18). Through one man's disobedience (Adam), sin entered into the world and death by sin, but through one man's obedience (Jesus) we receive the gift of righteousness.

Romans 5:14 refers to what is called the Law of Inclusion. Hebrews 7:9-10 helps us understand this better. It states that when Abraham paid tithes to Melchisedec, Levi, who although was four generations away, also paid tithes. How so? Because in the loins of Abraham was Isaac, Jacob, Joseph, and the twelve tribes of Israel of which Levi was one. So because Levi was in Abraham when he (Abraham) reached out his hands to pay tithes, Levi also paid tithes. Likewise, when Adam sinned, there in him was our great, great, great, great, grandfather, of whose loins we were (see also 1 Corinthians 15:22). So when we were born on this earth, before we committed our first sin, we were already sinners, not based on what we did, but based on our nature.

Second Corinthians 5:21 explains the awesomeness of God's plan of redemption. *"For he hath made him to be sin for us, who knew no sin; that we might be made the righteousness of God in him."*

Now, we see why the enemy attacked Jesus' emotions. He understood that if Jesus endured the death of the cross, man would be brought back into right standing with God (the true meaning of righteousness); that sin would be abolished.

> *"The next day John seeth Jesus coming unto him, and saith, Behold the Lamb of God, which taketh away the sin of the world"(John 1:29).*

Thank God Jesus did not give in to his emotions on Calvary. His obedience brought man back into harmony with God, resuming God's original plan for man (Genesis 1:26).

Every believer must get a revelation of this. Because of what Jesus did, our lives have been redeemed from destruction (Galatians 3:13). He re-purchased us (Matthew 20:28), not with money; there was not enough money in the Federal Reserve, the U.S. Mint or Fort Knox to purchase us; we were too valuable. The only thing God could find valuable enough to purchase us from sin was the pure, untainted blood of Jesus (Hebrews 7:25-28; Hebrews 9:12-15; 1 Peter 1:18-19). The curse has been removed. We no longer have to suffer with sickness, poverty, or death.

Now what does God expect? He expects us to be partakers in this plan of redemption. Note Second Peter 1:4:

> *"By means of these He has bestowed on us His precious and exceedingly great promises, so that through them you may escape [by flight] from the moral decay (rottenness and corruption) that is in the world because of covetousness (lust and greed), and become sharers (partakers) of the divine nature" (Amplified).*

And 1 Peter 4:12-13:

"Beloved, do not be amazed and bewildered at the fiery ordeal which is taking place to test your quality, as though something strange (unusual and alien to you and your position) were befalling you. But insofar as you are sharing Christ's sufferings, rejoice, so that when His glory [full of radiance and splendor] is revealed, you may also rejoice with triumph [exultantly]" (Amplified).

What did he just say? To partake means to take your part in Christ's sufferings. Christ became sin on the cross. When he did, you became righteous. Christ was wounded so that you could be made whole—totally healed; he was wounded so you could walk in perfect health. The Bible states in 2 Corinthians 8:9 that Jesus became poor that through his poverty we might be rich. Look at the parts. His part was to get sick; my part is to stay healthy. I am not going to get sick for the Lord. He does not want me to get sick for Him. He wants me to resist sickness and partake in the health that He's provided. His part was to become sin, my part is to accept my righteousness; His part was to become poor, and my part is to be rich. What happens when we misinterpret "partakers of His suffering"? Some believers translate this as God allowing them to suffer because He's testing them; He is trying to teach them something. Is this scriptural; is this the heart of a loving Father? God is not trying to teach you something, the devil is trying to kill you and you need to wake up. There is no credit for that. Jesus suffered so that you wouldn't have to suffer. He became poor so that you could be made perpetually rich. You shouldn't be climbing up the rough side of the mountain—that's a heavy burden. Your burdens are supposed to be light (Matthew 11:28-30). You are supposed to be rejoicing all the time, not experiencing the spirit of heaviness, but full of praise and thanksgiving.

You must see yourself the way that God does. Your salvation came at a very expensive cost. There is absolutely nothing [nothing] separating you from enjoying the abundant life (spirit, soul, and body) except a sin-consciousness, a victim mentality. Romans 3:23 says that although this life is available for all, it will only be manifested in the lives of those who will receive it. Galatians 4:1 says, *"Now I say, That the heir, as a long as he is a child, differeth nothing from a servant, though he be lord of all."* In other words, although you have been positioned to inherit the world and the God kind of life, until you get understanding, you will continue to live as a servant; a servant to poverty and sickness, which includes depression and death. Depression is no longer a mystery. Therefore, you don't have to be enslaved to it another day. He has turned my mourning into dancing, come join the celebration. Life is so good.

My Charge to You:

ARISE [from the depression and prostration in which circumstances have kept you—rise to a new life]! Shine (be radiant with the glory of the Lord), for your light has come, and the glory of the Lord has risen upon you! *(Isaiah 60:1, Amplified)*

The Worm Has Spun Her Cocoon *10*

❧❧❧

*T*HE SPIRIT of the Lord God is upon me, because the Lord has anointed and qualified me to preach the Gospel of good tidings to the meek, the poor, and afflicted; He has sent me to bind up and heal the brokenhearted, to proclaim liberty to the [physical and spiritual] captives and the opening of the prison and of the eyes to those who are bound, [To proclaim the acceptable year of the Lord [the year of His favor] and the day of vengeance of our God, to comfort all who mourn, To grant [consolation and joy] to those who mourn in Zion—to give them an ornament (a garland or diadem) of beauty instead of ashes, the oil of joy instead of mourning, the garment [expressive] of praise instead of a heavy, burdened, and failing spirit—that they may be called oaks of righteousness [lofty, strong, and magnificent, distinguished for uprightness, justice, and right standing with God], the planting of the Lord, that He may be glorified" (Isaiah 61:1-3, Amplified).*

When I was first called into the ministry, I wore a beautiful white robe with Isaiah 61:1 inscribed on the back of it. I did not realize until writing the climax to this book, that it was a seed that the Lord had given me that has manifested some twenty-three years later.

Luke's account of Isaiah 61:1 says, *"The Spirit of the Lord [is] upon Me, because He has anointed Me [the Anointed one, the Messiah] to preach the good news (the Gospel) to the poor; He has sent Me to announce release to the captives and recovery of sight to the blind, to send forth as delivered those who are oppressed [who are downtrodden, bruised, crushed, and broken down by calamity], To proclaim the accepted and acceptable year of the Lord [the day when salvation and the free favors of God profusely abound]" (Luke 4:18-19, Amplified).*

Notice he said, He sends us forth as delivered. The problem with some preachers, as was my problem, is we are going forth without first being delivered. I preached for some sixteen years with that crippling spirit of depression ruling my life. Although many lives were being changed as a result of my ministry, I was not a partaker of the fruit and God could not get maximum benefit from me. I was a miserable, miserable soul.

Thank God those pills didn't work; thank God that cold barrel of the .357 Magnum frightened me so much I couldn't pull the trigger; thank God for sending me a Godly man full of faith who vehemently refused to minister to my emotions. Had these variables been any different, you would not be reading this life-changing book.

I know you want to know. Everyone asks the proverbial question: "Dr. Moss, do you ever get depressed?" The answer is NO, Emphatically and Unequivocally NO! I won't allow it. Matthew 12:43-45 says *"When the unclean spirit is gone out of a man, he walketh through dry places, seeking rest, and findeth none. Then he saith, I will return into my house from whence I came out; and when he is come, he findeth it empty, swept, and garnished. Then goeth he, and taketh with himself seven other spirits more wicked than himself, and they enter in and dwell there: and the last state of that man is worse than the first."*

I want nothing to do with this demonic spirit or his cousins, fear, doubt, unbelief, suicide, and murder. Remember this is Satan's ultimate goal (John 10:10). Does he seek re-entry" Of course. There are times when I feel depression approaching, but I have trained myself not to be moved by my feelings. The scripture says to *"Withstand him; be firm in faith [against **his onset**—rooted, established, strong, immovable, and determined]..." (1 Peter 5:9, Amplified).* When I sense its presence, I pray in the spirit and immediately start reminding myself who I am through my confessions of faith.

No Condemnation

Depression carries with it such a negative stigma because we are taught to be unmovable and no matter what the circumstances, we should be able to "snap out of it." We also feel that we are alone and no one would understand our dilemma. God forbid if we are in leadership. What would people say? So we hide behind these walls not realizing that we are barricading ourselves in with an enemy. We are not ignorant of the devil's devices. First Peter 5:9 goes on to say "knowing that the same (identical) sufferings are appointed to your brotherhood (the whole body of Christians) throughout the world" (Amplified). So, you are not alone. Since writing this book, I've talked to **many** who have self-disclosed about their battle with this oppressive spirit, most of whom are believers. Without the Word of God, and an entire renewal of your mind, it is impossible to defeat this tried and tested foe. The grip is too strong. Seize your victory with the information revealed in this book and by getting free from condemnation.

"THEREFORE, [there is] now no condemnation (no adjudging guilty of wrong) for those who are in Christ Jesus, who live [and] walk not after the dictates of the flesh, but after the dictates of the Spirit. For the law of the Spirit of life [which is] in Christ Jesus [the law of our new being] has freed me from the law of sin and of death" (Romans 8:1-2, Amplified).

It is important that you do not walk in condemnation; it affects your confidence toward God. Look at what 1 John 3:20-21 has to say about this, however, let's read it in reverse order,

Verse 21: "And, beloved, if our consciences (our hearts) do not accuse us [if they do not make us feel guilty and condemn us], we have confidence (complete assurance and boldness) before God, Whenever our hearts in [tormenting] self-accusation make us feel guilty and condemn us" (Amplified).
Verse 20: "[For we are in God's hands.] For He is above and greater than our consciences (our hearts), and He knows (perceives and understands) everything [nothing is hidden from Him]" (Amplified).

If your heart condemns you, God is greater than your heart. You have no reason to feel shame or guilt. Likewise, don't let anyone put you under condemnation for going to the doctors or for taking medication. You must operate at your level of faith, but don't stay on that level forever. Continue in God's Word until you develop faith in the healing power of God's Word. Depression is only one of the weapons the enemy will use against you; our goal is to remove them all.

Finally, don't allow the enemy to be your accuser; this is now your past. The Apostle Paul in his own words admitted to molesting the church (Acts 22:4, 26:11; 1 Corinthians 15:9); however, although virtually a terrorist, when he gave his life to Christ his testimony was, "I've wronged no man." Note 2 Corinthians 7:2, *"Do open your hearts to us again [enlarge them to take us in]. We have wronged no one, we have betrayed or corrupted no one, we have cheated or taken advantage of no one).* He understood redemption.

Don't waste another minute. Take back your life. Not only is God waiting for you to manifest His kingdom, all creation is saying, "Will the real sons of God please stand up?" People in the world (your relatives, co-workers, etc.) really want to see someone different than they are. The world cannot be converted until they see the manifestation of God in our lives. They need to see that it pays to serve God.

"All creation is waiting for the manifestation of the sons of God" (Romans 8:19).

"Look well to yourself [to your own personality] and to [your] teaching; persevere in these things [hold to them], for by so doing you will save both yourself and those who hear you. (1 Tim 4:16)

My life is proof that the information revealed in this book works. My life has completely changed. I am complete in Christ and have connected to eternal purpose. My language has changed, my appearance has changed (I am 54 pounds lighter); my heart has changed and now I am sent forth as delivered. The reason I live is to affect change in the lives of people, so they can be free to be who God has created them to be. This is my first thought of the day and my last one at night. I am like a butterfly, beautiful and free. My life is like a dream. I am literally living days of heaven right here on earth. I never knew life could be so good. You can too. It's your right.

Second Timothy 2:24-26 captures so well, the epitome of this book:

> *"And the servant of the Lord must correct his opponents with courtesy and gentleness, in the hope that God may grant that they will repent and come to know the Truth [that they will perceive and recognize and become accurately acquainted with and acknowledge it], And that they may come to their senses [and] escape out of the snare of the devil, having been held captive by him, [Henceforth] to do His [God's] will" (Amplified).*

A Word to Non-believers:

If you are not a believer (have not accepted Jesus Christ into your heart), let me take this opportunity to invite you into the family of God so you too can enjoy this good life. This book has revealed what the life of God provides—total life prosperity. But, it is only promised to those in the family of God.

It's quite simple, just repeat the sinner's prayer and Jesus (God's Son) will come and make His permanent dwelling in your heart. Don't waste another minute; don't ask another question. If you are not born again, you will continue to live a life well beneath that which the Lord has predestined for you. Make a radical decision today to change your life by committing your heart to the Lord. Simply repeat this prayer:

> *Heavenly Father, I come to You in the Name of Jesus. Your Word says, "Whosoever shall call on the name of the Lord shall be saved" (Acts 2:21). I am calling on You. I pray and ask Jesus to come into my heart and be Lord over my life according to Romans 10:9-10, "If thou shalt confess with thy mouth the Lord Jesus, and shalt believe in thine heart that God hath raised him from the dead, thou shalt be saved." I*

do that now. I confess that Jesus is Lord, and I believe in my heart that God raised Him from the dead. From now on from this day forward I belong to you, in the name of Jesus.

Appendix

PRESCRIPTION FOR THE GOD KIND OF LIFE

(NO HARMFUL SIDE-EFFECTS)

1. Invite Jesus into your heart. Repeat the sinner's prayer at the end of this book and Jesus will take His place on the throne of your heart. The Holy Spirit will join Him to lead and guide you into all truth—the truth of God's Word and what it has to say about you (Romans 10:10; John 14:26; 16:13).

2. Join or ensure you attend a Word of Faith church that teaches the Word of God; not that teaches *about* the Word, but that teaches *the Word*. Your faith must be developed and faith comes by hearing and hearing by the Word of God (Romans 10:8-17).

3. Ensure you have a daily supply of the Word of God. Flood your entry points (eyes and ears) with the Word. You can read the Word, but you can also listen to the Word. We have no excuses because the internet, one of the wonders of God, is available 24 hours a day. You can listen to anointed teaching and satu-

rate your soul with life-changing Word. There is, of course, also CD's and DVD's available on the Anointed Word. Invest in your life; purchase these resources to renew your mind.

4. Meditate on the Word daily. It's the way you change what you believe (Joshua 1:8; 2 Timothy 3:16).

5. Speak the Word only—that is watch what you say; the law of confession is at work all the time (Matthew 8:8; Romans 10:8; 2 Corinthians 4:13).

6. Develop and employ a daily confession list. Jesus found Himself in the Scripture; you too can find yourself. Find out what God says about you and the abundant life and write down the scriptures, then begin to confess these scriptures (out loud) over you and your family as often as necessary (Mark 11:22-24; Romans 4:17).

7. Build yourself up by praying in the Holy Ghost. The more you do this, you'll have the same testimony as Smith Wigglesworth, who said by confessing 1 John 4:4, "I realized I'm a thousand times bigger on the inside than I am on the outside" (Jude 20, 1 Corinthians 14:2). Smith Wigglesworth is accounted for raising more people from the dead than anyone in Christendom.

8. Have an active prayer life. Your fellowship with God is essential. You cannot make it without this fellowship. Your life depends on it (Matthew 6:9-15; 26:41; Luke 18:1). This is how you develop

your trust in Him. Set up a schedule to spend quality time with God in prayer.

9. Flee corrupt associations. It is interesting that another word for associations is mental link. It matters who you have as associates. You must surround yourself with "faith" people; people who believe this Word is true so they can "jack you up" when necessary and keep you on course. Don't be afraid to separate yourself from unbelieving believers, who constantly speak words of doubt and unbelief. It could get into your field (heart) and stop your harvest (Proverbs 11:14, 13:20; Mark 4:14-20; 1 Cor.15:33).

10. Repeat steps 1-9 as often as necessary; they carry no harmful side effects and if taken as prescribed, the prognosis is irrefutable; total life prosperity.

For teaching tapes from Dr. Moss or to
request her ministry gift at your church or next
conference, please call or write us at:

Repairers of the Breach Ministries
P.O. Box 911
Smithfield, VA 23431
(757) 356-9727

Or visit us on the World Wide Web at
www.soteriacci.org

CPSIA information can be obtained at www.ICGtesting.com
Printed in the USA
LVOW12s1107190913

353199LV00001B/12/A

9 781602 668232